PETROC

Becoming an Effective Teacher

PAUL STEPHENS AND TIM CRAWLEY

Text © Paul Stephens and Tim Crawley 1994

First published in 1994 by:
Stanley Thornes (Publishers) Ltd

Reprinted in 2002 by:
Nelson Thornes Ltd
Delta Place
27 Bath Road
CHELTENHAM
GL53 7TH
United Kingdom

02 03 04 05 06 / 15 14 13 12 11 10 9 8 7 6

A catalogue record for this book is available from the British Library

ISBN 0 7487 1935 0

Page make-up by Merle and Alan Thompson

Printed and bound in Great Britain by Ashford Colour Press Ltd

Contents

FOREWORD

There is no doubt that the Department for Education's criteria for the development of competencies, during a course of initial teacher training, have had a marked impact on the design and delivery of teacher training courses, and will have a continuing influence for many years to come. This book offers a refreshing and readable account of what this all means for student teachers, and how they can best think about their own progress and development in terms of these competencies during their teacher training. Paul Stephens and Tim Crawley have put their understanding of the nature of teaching, and the key tasks involved, to good effect and produced a book that will be of immense help to student teachers. It deserves to be widely read.

Dr Chris Kyriacou
University of York
May 1994

ACKNOWLEDGEMENTS

The authors wish to thank all those colleagues, friends and family who have helped and encouraged us during the writing of this book. In particular, we would like to thank Paul Hirst for his National Curriculum updates, Dave Bennett for his expertise about Special Needs, Indru Nariani for his input on Science and Anne Forgham for her insight about assessment.

T C & P S

Dedications

To my father, who persuaded me to become a teacher, and to my mother, who encouraged me to write about being a teacher.

P S

To Victoria for everything – again. To Michael for his friendship and bad puns. To Jenny, Trevor, Owen, David, Maria and all at Guppy's. To mum and dad: thank you.

T C

And finally, to our students, who have given us the reason and material to write this book. Thank you for helping us to become effective teachers.

T C & P S

PREFACE

First, let us introduce ourselves. When we first wrote this book in 1994, we worked in a large, northern comprehensive school in a former mining community. In the main text, the present tense is still used, even though, as indicated below, our careers have moved on.

Paul, the 'elder statesman' of the two, had been at the 'chalkface' for fifteen years, having taught in primary as well as secondary schools. He was then Head of Social Sciences and also a school-based teacher educator (mentor) working with student teachers from a nearby university. Paul taught sociology and history.

Tim entered teaching in 1990 after a very successful career as a 'troubleshooter' in the computer industry. He was and still is involved in school-based teacher education. Tim taught English and psychology, and was the school's Computer Support Manager. We were both form tutors as well as subject teachers, so we know a thing or two about pastoral and curriculum issues.

In 1996, Paul left teaching to concentrate on educational research and writing. He is now associate professor of education at the Institute of Pedagogy, Stavanger College, Norway. In 1995, Tim took up a post as an English teacher in a local comprehensive school. He also still teachers psychology.

In this book, we want to make available to you, the intending teacher, the distilled wisdom of our craft knowledge, as well as some important insights extracted from educational research.

Given that the Department for Education and Employment (DfEE) wants to raise the level of professional skills of new teachers by linking Initial Teacher Education more closely to classroom practice, *Becoming an Effective Teacher* is a timely guide. As two experienced teachers, we have kept apace of contemporary trends in schools and the book targets the professional competence standards set out by the DfEE for the education of tomorrow's teachers.

Extracting the main gist of these criteria – which despite some rubric amendments in 1997, remain essentially as they first were in 1992 – we put the information into direct, easy to understand language, and address the skills that will endure long after any further subsequent tinkering with the DfEE directives. *Becoming an Effective Teacher* provides expert, practitioner-derived advice and guidance on how best to accomplish the required professional expertise in the classroom. Our counsel is also based on some of the most recent research findings from studies of school effectiveness and school improvement.

Given that there are two writers, 'I' and 'we' are both used in this book to illustrate individual and common experiences, respectively. We hope that this does not cause too much confusion, and we urge you not to worry about which author is writing when 'I' appears in the text. More importantly we hope this book will offer you constructive suggestions and practical strategies on how to develop the knowledge and skills that underpin good professional practice.

Tim Crawley and Paul Stephens
York and Stavanger
September 1998

1998 update

The Department for Education (DfE)
From July, 1995, this body acquired additional responsibilities, becoming the Department for Education and Employment (DfEE).

National Curriculum
From September 1995, Level Descriptions replaced Statements and Levels of Attainment. What this means is that 'best fit' descriptions of attainment against which students' performances can be matched are in, and 'tick box' performance indicators are out. This is good news for teachers who favour rounded judgements over mechanistic assessment.

At the end of Key Stages 1, 2 and 3, for all subjects except art, music, and physical education, standards of students' performances are defined by eight level descriptions of increasing difficulty. There is an additional description above level 8 that enables teachers to differentiate exceptional performance. For art, music and physical education, end of key stage descriptions define the standard of performance expected of the majority of students at the end of each Key Stage. Descriptions of exceptional performance are also provided in art and music at the end of Key Stage 3, and in physical education at the end of Key Stage 4. At Key Stage 4, public exams are the main means of assessing student performance in the National Curriculum.

We will clarify matters by describing Level Description 7 of English Attainment Target 1, Speaking and Listening (by the end of Key Stage 3, the performance of the majority of students 'should' be in the 3–7 range):

> *Pupils are confident in matching their talk to the demands of different contexts. They use vocabulary precisely and organise their talk to communicate clearly. In discussion, pupils make significant contributions, evaluating others' ideas and varying how and when they participate. They show confident use of standard English in situations that require it.*

Using this Level Description, a teacher might say: "I've taught Kazuko for a year, and in my professional judgement, her speaking and listening skills fit the description for Level 7".

Standard for the Award of Qualified Teacher Status
From September 1997, these standards replaced the more general competencies set out in DfE Circular 9/92. Essentially, the rubric has changed somewhat, but the 9/92 competencies are more or less intact. The 'Standards' refer to 'Standards of competence'. We generally use the term competence(s) for short.

Becoming an effective teacher

We thought about calling this book – A Survivor's Guide to Teaching. Staffroom culture, with its brisk, taut humour and frequent quips about joining the 'escape committee', evokes titles like that. So too does the look on those tired, punished faces – the teachers', not the school students' – on a Friday afternoon.

But don't be put off. What other job offers you the chance to inspire people in their quest for knowledge or to shape the citizen outlook of tomorrow's adults? Not many. How many occupations invite you to make a difference? The title did not fit.

When things go right in teaching, it's hard to think of a more satisfying job. Yet sadly, intending teachers are sometimes worried that today's young people are too tough to handle. The embers of this understandable but actually unfounded fear are aggressively fanned by exaggerated media accounts of 'classroom warriors' on the rampage.

Even though, working at the chalkface in a 1990s, comprehensive secondary school sometimes makes us feel in need of survival strategies, that feeling, thankfully, is fairly infrequent. Teaching has its share of stress, but so do most jobs. Moreover, causes and perceptions of stress vary considerably between different teachers.

Contrary to vivid tabloid scaremongering, 'heavy-duty thuggery' on

1

the part of school students is a very rare source of teacher stress. According to research carried out by David A. Gillborn, Jon Nixon and Jean Rudduck (1988), the most common cause of teacher stress is low-level disruptive behaviour on the part of some, but certainly not all, students.

These are the kind of student antics so brilliantly and amusingly captured by the sociologist, Paul Willis, in his book, *Learning to Labour* (1988):

> Settled in class, as near a group as they (the disruptive students) can manage, there is a continuous scraping of chairs ... and a continuous fidgeting about which explores every permutation of sitting or lying on a chair .... There is an aimless air of insubordination ready with spurious justification and impossible to nail down.

So how do good teachers deal with such authority-threatening behaviour? We'll come to that in due course. Suffice it to say at this stage, that a recently published book by Ted Wragg (1993) based on one of the largest studies of teaching skills ever undertaken in English primary schools (much of the research findings apply to good practice in secondary schools), concluded that: 'Children prefer teachers to be slightly strict, explain things clearly, use rewards and punishments in a fair-minded manner, and have a sense of humour.'

True to the spirit of our opening paragraph though, we do not want to over-emphasise the need for 'coping' strategies. Teaching can be fun. It can also be very rewarding, less though in financial than in job satisfaction terms. Do not be misled by exaggerated accounts of the alleged 'Bash Street' habits of the 1990s secondary school student.

Most of the students in the school where we teach behave far more courteously than do politicians during parliamentary debates. Many of them also show a great deal more concern about human suffering and social justice than the politicians. So do not think that effective teaching depends on acquiring the custodial know-how of a San Quentin prison guard, and on holding potentially recalcitrant students in check. Few teachers these days would measure their professional effectiveness on the basis of keeping classroom rebellion at bay.

Being an effective teacher means being able to get the best out of your students, measured in terms of educational, psychological and social outcomes. To put this in simple terms, if your teaching and your interactive style contribute to improvement on those three important fronts, you are doing your job well.

This book will help you to become an effective teacher. If you already are an effective teacher, you'll find advice and guidance – much of it culled from our own tried and tested teaching methods – that will help you to become even better at your job.

The emphasis throughout is on contemporary issues, most notably, current Department of Education (DfE) initiatives on competence-based teacher education. Those initiatives are described and explained in simple, straightforward language, and constructive suggestions are offered on how teachers can work conscientiously within the new system. Incidentally, the terms 'teacher education' and 'teacher training' are used interchangeably in this book. We prefer 'education', but the DfE are more inclined to use 'training'.

Becoming an Effective Teacher looks at what's good and what works. It presents a set of strategies for teachers to use in the classroom. The strategies will enhance your effectiveness by showing you how to stretch your students' intellects, how to stroke their egos, and how to nurture their sociability.

The book will be useful to student teachers, newly-qualified teachers, and teachers returning to the chalkface after some years' gap. It might also be of interest to more experienced teachers who want to keep up with new research and recent developments in secondary school practice. Teacher educators, whether university or school-based, will probably find the book helpful as well. So, too, will anyone who is interested in what is going on in the nation's schools today.

While what follows is linked to secondary school teaching, there is much in the book that will be of benefit to primary school teachers and (dare we say it?) to teachers in higher education. My own teaching portfolio is wide-reaching: it embraces seven years in secondary schools, six years in primary schools, two years in teacher education (primary), two years abroad in child and adult TEFL, and one year as an 'all-ages' swimming instructor.

Although I work in a comprehensive secondary school at the moment, my experiences in inner-city primary schools equipped me with valuable, transferable knowledge and competencies which I now use to good effect in my dealings with older students. Being a primary school teacher taught me that what matters most to students, whatever their age, has less to do with what you teach and more to do with how you make your subject(s) compelling, enjoyable and understandable.

In short, good teaching has more to do with style than with content. Good style elevates teaching above the level of mere drill and rote. It captures the fleeting regard of students, holds their attention, grabs their interest, entertains them, and wins their enduring confidence.

But what has this book got to offer that some other books do not already provide?

- It is written by well-experienced, currently serving teachers, one of whom is a head of department and a school-based teacher educator (a so-called mentor) to student teachers from a local university.
- It explicitly targets the most recent DfE Competences expected of Newly Qualified Teachers, as contained in DfE Circular 9/92, 25 June 1992: Initial Teacher Training (Secondary Phase), and it does this with reference to current research into good practice, as well as on the basis of the two authors' professionally derived experience.

A competence-based approach to teacher training

In order to simplify and sharpen the focus of what is to follow, we have dealt with each of the 'Competences' referred to above (five in all) under five separate chapter headings. The chapters are largely self-contained, so you can read them in any order you choose, or even omit those chapters that you might not wish to read.

To achieve its objective, the DfE requires the training establishments to, 'focus on the competences of teaching throughout the whole period of initial training'. It also stipulates that the 'progressive development of these competences should be monitored regularly during initial training', and that their 'attainment at a level appropriate to newly qualified teachers should be the objective of every student taking a course of initial training' (DfE, 1992).

Let us put this into plain English. The DfE requires the new secondary school teacher to have acquired by the end of Initial Teacher Training (namely, the period of training prior to becoming a Newly Qualified Teacher), a portfolio of professional competences. The institution where you receive your training is therefore obliged to furnish you with a course that will enable you to harness and develop those competences.

So what are the competences? The DfE has specified five of them, each containing appropriate sub-section components. We do not want to get too technical at the moment, so at this stage we will just list the umbrella competences, together with very brief summaries of what they mean.

1 Subject Knowledge: know your subject well.
2 Subject Application: teach your subject well.
3 Class Management: teach your subject in a purposeful, orderly environment which promotes effective learning.
4 Assessment and Recording of Pupils' Progress: identify your students' levels of attainment and keep systematic records of their performances.
5 Further Professional Development: realise that Initial Teacher Training is the first stage of a process of continued training that will proceed throughout your professional career.

This is not, however, the full story. The DfE has decided that the above competences do not purport to offer a complete syllabus for the would-be-teacher. There's more to come: like learning how to avoid doing an end-of-school bus duty on a Friday afternoon (I recently failed miserably on that criterion), how to participate in a free school trip to France even though you're not a modern languages teacher (I recently succeeded on that criterion), and so on!

On a more serious note though, the designated competences will form the main criteria against which your teaching skills will be assessed. So where do you go from here? A good start would be to read this book.

Chapter 1, *The new chalkface teaching*, describes, explains and puts into context the DfE's policy of bringing more teacher training into classrooms. Chapters 2–6, *Knowing your subject, Teaching your subject, Class management, Assessing and recording*, and *Professional development*, each focus on one of the five DfE Competences – extracting their central tenets, putting them into simple language, and suggesting how to put them into effective practice. Each of these five chapters concludes with a *What your mentor should do for you* section, focusing on observation and practice tasks (bear in mind that the two often overlap), followed by a series of summative 'Action points'. Chapter 7, *Looking ahead*, offers important advice about seeking appointments, assesses the impact of current educational reforms on the teacher's role, spells out some of the ramifications of the 'electronic classroom', and examines important implications of school effectiveness and school improvement research for modern classroom practice.

In its drive to raise the level of professional skill of new teachers, the DfE is making explicit what experienced teachers have long been doing implicitly. This means that the craft-based insights which underpin *Becoming an Effective Teacher* will still be relevant and useful even if, at some later time, the DfE Competences are removed or replaced.

That said, the current skills-based criteria are likely to endure for quite a while. The genie is out of the bottle and it is on almost every educational agenda. While it is fair to say the Competences seem to be over-prescriptive, they nevertheless do articulate routine practices in ways that might help student teachers, beginning teachers, and, who knows, perhaps some seasoned veterans, to make sense of what goes on, and, more importantly, what should go on in classrooms.

Once the Competences have been identified and translated by us into plain English, we then suggest ways in which you might try to implement them. Our proposals are not based on hearsay or half-truths. They are derived from our personal stock of professional-craft knowledge, from our observations of exemplary practice among successful primary, secondary and higher education teaching colleagues, and from the stockpiled insights of good research.

However, before moving on to a more detailed examination of the Competences and to advice on how best to acquire and deploy them, it's useful first to consider three of the recurrent themes that underpin the DfE's thinking. These are matters that have an important bearing on what's expected of tomorrow's teachers. The themes are:

- School-based teacher training
- National Curriculum and National Assessment
- The 'market model' of school administration.

School-based teacher training

The DfE is placing more emphasis on school-based 'skills acquisition' in Initial Teacher Training than on campus-style 'intellectual theorising'. In short, you will spend more time these days honing your craft skills at the chalkface than studying the 'ologies' in a lecture-hall.

The shift from the allegedly book-oriented nature of higher education-based study to the supposedly practically concerned focus of school-located training was given added momentum in January 1992, when the then Secretary of State for Education, Kenneth Clarke, announced that secondary Initial Teacher Training should be increasingly provided in schools.

This proposal was tested in a 1993–4 pilot scheme whereby selected schools received the full DfE funding for Initial Teacher Training, buying in, if they wished, the expertise of educational departments in higher education institutes. If the DfE declares the pilot scheme a success, it is conceivable that the educating of future student teachers will eventually become entirely located in schools.

As practising teachers who are both involved in school-based training, we believe that higher education institutes and schools have equally important roles to play in the education of tomorrow's teachers. The suggestion by some commentators that the higher education component of Initial Teacher Training has abstracted out of 'real' educational issues is simply not true. On the contrary, unleashing 'raw recruits' into modern classrooms without first providing them insights derived from the latest university research into 'class management', is not a helpful strategy. The 'sink or swim' approach is dangerously ill-informed and bad for both trainee teachers and school students.

Remember, too, that we make this assertion not as university tutors, but as 'chalk-on-the hands' practitioners who provide on-the-job instruction to student teachers. If the current move towards more school-focused teacher training is to yield benefits to future teachers, it must be achieved by wedding the obvious gains of craft-based practice with the direct access to healthy, intellectual debate and to research that higher education institutes continue to provide.

National Curriculum and National Assessment

An important feature of DfE policy is its statutory introduction of a National Curriculum and a national system of standardised assessment criteria for all students aged 5–16 attending state sector schools in England and Wales. Under the Subject Knowledge Competence, newly qualified teachers should acquire, 'knowledge and understanding of the National Curriculum and attainment targets ... in the subjects they are preparing to teach, together with an understanding of the framework of the statutory requirements'. With this Competence installed, teachers are presumably equipped to handle the Assessment and Recording of Pupils' Progress Competence, namely, that they should know how to 'identify the current level of attainment of individual pupils using National Curriculum and Attainment Targets, statements of attainment and end of key stage statements where applicable'.

Putting this into simple terms: teachers of National Curriculum subjects who teach students aged 5–16, are required by law to know and understand what to teach and how to assess their students' progress.

Let's not get too caught up though in the ever-changing complexities of the National Curriculum. Suffice it to say that 'ever-changing' have been the operative words up until very recently. The National Curriculum is still being phased in, and it's likely to be modified, though not drastically, in the years to come. This book focuses on those parts of the National Curriculum that are likely to remain in place.

A market model of school administration

The DfE is actively promoting a market-oriented approach to state-sector schooling. In that context, schools are being provided with the statutory wherewithal to control most (Local Management of Schools) or all (Grant Maintained Status) of their delegated budgets. We work in a Locally Managed comprehensive school which has 1800 students, and the current (1993–4) annual budget is about three and a half million pounds. Local Management of Schools in the Local Education Authority where we teach, means that our school will control about 87 per cent of this amount: some three million pounds. That is a lot of money. The fact that teachers are directly involved in financial decision-making on a bigger scale than previously, has meant that the language of the market-place is becoming increasingly more commonplace in schools.

Don't be surprised to hear of heads of department being referred to as 'line managers', or of the 'art of teaching' being described as 'delivering the curriculum'. Call us old-fashioned if you will, but we still describe ourselves as 'teachers who teach'. That said, we nevertheless have to accept that there are far more administrative, financial and so-called 'managerial' duties than in the past. And that trend looks set to continue.

So brush up your Information Technology (IT) skills, especially word-processing, spread-sheeting and data-basing, and get to work on basic account-keeping, if you want to rise rapidly in the 'market culture' of your future work-place. Even though, like us, you might not feel comfortable with the new ethos, you won't lose out by becoming computer-literate: if only not to have to compromise your 'Teacher of the Year 2000' credibility in the eyes of your students, many of whom are likely to be into personal computers in a big way.

Linked to the market model, is the DfE emphasis on 'accountability'. The 'name of the game' is Total Quality Assurance (TQA). In short, keep the 'customer' happy by providing her or him with unassailable evidence that your school comes out, respectively, 'top' and 'bottom', in terms of national league tables of public examination results and truancy rates. Make sure, too, that you or your head of department has your Departmental Handbook ready for the new Office for Standards in Education (OFSTED) inspectors when they come knocking on the doors of your school. Their first inspections began in September 1993.

They will be paying you and your school a visit on a regular four-year cycle. The OFSTED inspectors require a great deal of 'pre-inspection' documentation (notably, on how your department plans to 'deliver' and assess its planned curriculum). This data will provide hypotheses (the 'issues for inspection') that the inspectors will test during their on-site inspection. So it pays to get sharp and smart in the record-keeping parts of your teacher education.

Effective teaching

It's important, however, to recognise that effective teaching can never just be about impressive documentation. Being an effective teacher is judged ultimately in terms of imparting knowledge and values that students can comprehend and relate to. We won't summon statistics to help us at this stage, but we can call to the witness stand many years' professional experience when we claim that effective teaching is about:

- unashamedly loving your subject and getting your students to know that you love it
- making your subject exciting, and linking it, wherever possible, to issues that your students can relate to in their real world
- making complex issues understandable

- asking questions that elicit evaluative or imaginative answers
- listening to your students, and thereby avoiding too much 'chalk and talk'
- setting work that your students can realistically handle
- marking your students' work 'sympathetically', always trying to include some 'success at task' praise and returning the work promptly
- starting off kind and staying kind rather than believing in the 'start off tough' maxim
- showing your students that you care about them, not just as learners, but as people
- being impeccably courteous to your students, even (we know it's hard) when they're not being even slightly courteous to you
- having a sense of humour without being unduly jolly
- challenging, with due sensitivity, racism, sexism and all the other negative '-isms'
- framing and acting on your humanity within the opportunities and the constraints of the authentic culture of the school and the community in which you work
- staying long enough, if possible, in the same school for student 'folk-lore' to establish the reputation you deservedly want to earn (doing things well in public, for example, successfully entertaining all of Year 10 in an Assembly, will greatly enhance your student-perceived status)
- realising that Initial Teacher Training is only one phase in your long-term professional development.

After compiling the above list, we were later encouraged to read that recently published research into effective teaching, by Sally Brown and Donald McIntyre (1993), found that 12 and 13-year-old students in a city comprehensive school who were asked to appraise their teachers, reported that good teachers:

- created a relaxed and enjoyable atmosphere in the classroom
- did not lose their 'cool' when exercising control
- presented their subject in an interesting and engaging manner
- made lessons understandable
- gave clear instructions of what to do and what students should try to achieve
- set work that students could reasonably achieve

- helped students with difficulties
- encouraged students to raise their expectations of themselves
- cared about students and treated them as mature individuals
- had certain 'star-quality' talents (subject-related or other).

We were pleased to see that many of the qualities valued by these students did figure in our priorities. More about these and other effective teaching strategies later. Meanwhile, during your 'apprenticeship' alongside school mentors, take every opportunity to ransack their chalkface experiences of how best to deal with both the expected and the unexpected events that occur in classrooms. For, as Hazel Hagger (1992) correctly writes:

> Learning to be a teacher means developing a stock of personal situational understandings. These consist of 'experienced cases which are stored in a practitioner's long term memory' and constitute the teacher's professional knowledge .... Making this repertoire available to the student teacher is a central task of mentoring ...'

Distilling the accumulated wisdom of good, experienced teachers by talking with them and watching them at their craft, and seeing if that knowledge works for you, is one of the best ways we know of becoming an effective teacher fast.

To access the best ingredients of professional craft knowledge, you need to persuade effective teachers to tell you what they prize most about their own teaching, what goals they set, and how they achieve these goals. This book seeks to make available to you those aspects of good practice which are generalisable and worthy of imitation. Emulating the competencies that classroom practice and classroom research demonstrate work well, is no bad thing.

It is hoped that *Becoming an Effective Teacher* will successfully convey to you some of the skills that work for the authors. It is also hoped the advice given will enable you to 'fine-tune' your training experiences in line with the competence criteria laid down by the DfE. Don't treat this book, however, as just another 'Teacher should ...' guide. Professional skills can't be reduced to simple 'rehearse-and-put-into-practice' drills. As Stanley Zehm and Jeffrey Kottler (1993) so rightly insist:

> ... all the knowledge and skills in the world are virtually useless to someone who cannot process their meaning in a personally designed

11

way or who cannot translate their value in a style that commands others' attention and influences their behaviour.

Your personality is bound to affect how you behave in the classroom. It's no good, for example, trying to mimic someone else's sense of humour. You might find out though that some of the things which make students smile are things that you can conjure up while still being honest to yourself. When you observe a practitioner skill that feels right for you, incorporate that skill into your memory and try it out when a suitable occasion arises. That's how you'll make the journey from being a mere observer to becoming an authentic practitioner.

The advice given is not prescriptive (even though much of the DfE criteria seem to be that way), nor is it exhaustive. We do hope though that we'll be able to help you to sharpen your focus. We also hope and think that you'll find this book enjoyable and stimulating to read.

This counsel will help you get the best out of your mentor.

What your mentor should do for you

Ask your mentor to:

- arrange plenty of opportunities for you to observe a wide range of teachers (newly qualified, seasoned veterans, tough disciplinarians, indulgent persuaders etc.) across different curriculum areas. The richer and more varied your watching brief, the better you'll be able to judge what will work for you
- provide you with the chance to see teachers working with students of varying ages, abilities and behaviours. Don't restrict yourself to looking at the kinds of student you think you'll be working with when you start teaching. Illustrative of that point, in one comprehensive school where I worked, I taught students in Years 7, 8, 9, 10, 11, 12 and 13, from low ability to high flyer, from conformist to rebel
- set up learning environments which give you optimum scope to cut your teeth on whole-class, group and individual teaching, as well as providing opportunities to go solo and to teach collaboratively. Don't see these options as either/or choices; regard them as components of a 'mixed tool-bag'. That way, your teaching will properly become more geared to specific circumstances, rather than uniformly unadaptable
- give you accurate, immediate feedback on your teaching and other

professional skills (like 'crowd control' in corridors, for instance). Tell your mentor not to pull any punches on the constructive criticism front, but expect her or him to also tell you what you're doing right.

One of the ways I, as a mentor, provide feedback is through lesson reports that adopt the format below. (Examples of the kinds of comment I make are included.)

Doing the right things

Great start. You welcomed the students as they entered the classroom, addressing many of them by name (they appreciate that personal touch), took the register straightaway (no time-wasting here), and began the lesson with some thought-provoking video clips (everything worked like clockwork: no fumbling around looking for the right cables).

Not doing the right things

Too little supportive and corrective feedback during the Question and Answer parts of the lesson. When students answer questions well, they expect and deserve praise. But don't hesitate to correct them if their answers are wide of the mark. Done with sensitivity ('Nice try Bob. You got the three part right, but Kennedy was assassinated in 1963, not 1973'), corrective feedback is a vital means of promoting effective learning.

Speaking of mentors, they play a leading role in the education of tomorrow's teachers. And they do most of their educating at the chalkface. The next chapter is therefore aptly titled – *The new chalkface training.*

CHAPTER 1

The new chalkface training

The DfE wants what student teachers learn today to be applied in the classroom tomorrow. It wants a closer match between the content of training and the competences necessary to carry out the job. Giving schools a stronger role in Initial Teacher Training is how it sees this goal being accomplished.

In its drive to switch more training from institutes and universities into schools, the DfE is pushing hard to ensure that schools shouldn't only act as full partners with higher education institutes, but should also be able – if they wish – to play the principal role in planning and providing courses.

Although some schools have signed up for full funding and control to run their own courses, DfE officials expect that school-based partnerships with higher education institutes will prove more popular than the school 'in the driving seat' model. Even if schools decide to go it alone, they may choose to buy certain services from the universities.

To quicken the pace of these new training initiatives, the Government is setting up a quango, the Teacher Training Agency, to fund the training of all student teachers in England. The Agency is to allocate funds to schools or higher education institutes that it judges will provide cost-effective, high quality Initial Teacher Training. Its principal port of call for advice on quality will be Her Majesty's Chief Inspector, who heads the Office for Standards in Education. The Agency will have a direct duty to foster school involvement in the educating of student teachers, and part of its budget is to be set aside for promoting that aim.

But how does all this affect you, the intending teacher? The short answer is, you will be spending more time in schools during your pre-service course than previous generations of student teachers. You will also be doing courses which place more emphasis on professional skills training – how to teach and how to maintain an orderly classroom – than on Educational Studies, which looks at how children learn and the nature and purpose of education.

In days gone by, there was a fairly straightforward division of labour between schools and higher education institutes: schools dealt with the practical side of things and the institutes handled theoretical issues. These days, the DfE want both partners in the training programme to keep the craft of teaching at the forefront.

The best way to turn raw recruits into confident class managers and effective teachers, according to the DfE, is to equip student teachers with the competencies necessary to do their future job well. Providers of Initial Teacher Training courses are therefore required to make sure that their intending teachers:

1 know their subject
2 are able to teach their subject
3 are able to run an orderly learning environment
4 can assess and record their students' progress
5 have a sufficiently secure basis on which to develop their knowledge and skills after entering the teaching profession.

These are the five DfE Competences referred to in the introduction to this book. They will form the main criteria against which your performance will be measured.

However, the new emphasis on 'real school issues', on skills training and on practical assessment is generating heated debate among educationists.

Critics of DfE policy fear the impending de-coupling of Initial

Teacher Training and higher education if schools are allowed to set up their own on-site Education Departments. In defence of their view that teacher education should remain wedded to the campus, the same critics argue that universities make a contribution which schools cannot provide: acquainting student teachers with the findings of recent research, encouraging a healthy scepticism about the latest fads and fashions in the educational world, and fostering a willingness to debate and ponder philosophical as well as practical issues.

If the educating of future teachers is handed over to serving teachers, claim the opponents of entirely school-located training, we shall get drill sergeants who know how to take attendance registers, how to supervise after-school detentions, how to control students in dining halls, and how to keep serried ranks of students occupied with chalk, talk and barked orders.

Against this argument, advocates of more or total school-based initiatives maintain that staffrooms are just as able as (if not better able than) senior common rooms to provide trainers whose qualifications and experience are well matched to the task of equipping intending teachers with the competencies necessary for effective practice. This view is held by a number of teachers involved in a pilot, school-led, training scheme launched in Kent in September 1993: the Bromley Schools' Collegiate Initial Teacher Training Programme.

The seven schools (all grant maintained) which make up the Collegiate, contend that higher education institutes have agendas which do not necessarily best promote teachers' interests. One of the teachers in the Collegiate raised the matter of the professional 'ownership' of training, noting that, 'The profession wants control of its own destiny'. A similar view was voiced by a Collegiate head teacher: 'Other professions issue their own qualifications. Why shouldn't we?' From the Collegiate's stand-point, the school-led scheme offers an opportunity to provide a professional culture rather than the student culture offered on university campuses (*The Times Educational Supplement*, 24 September 1993).

Schools are also well placed to research real educational issues in situ. After all, teachers are where the action is: in the classroom, in the playground, on the corridor. Their daily work involves handling matters that university tutors, with their alleged unreconstructed '70s views, can only theorise about in tutorials and seminars. Given that practical, school-based skills are what student teachers need if they're to behave like real teachers when they take up their first posts, is it not best to let real 'chalkface' practitioners take charge of the training? It is in the schools, not the universities, where the impact of authentic educational issues are felt and acted upon.

Hold on a moment. Aren't both sides exaggerating things here? Don't school educators (mentors) and university educators (tutors) both have something to offer the would-be teacher?

Mentors and tutors

With school-based immersion set to dominate professional training, the roles of the teacher educators are being redefined. Under the old system, university tutors taught the 'ologies on campus and supervised their students at the chalkface. School teachers were also involved in monitoring the practice side of things, and reported back to tutors on how the novices were shaping up. Tutors kept scholarship and idealism alive, but had a peculiar fondness for scripted lesson plans; school teachers emphasised know-how and realism and the merits of unscripted repartee. Student teachers tried to retain as much humanity as was consistent with what they learnt in college and what they faced with 11B on the rampage.

So where do we go from here? Under the new arrangements, the scripts are still being written. By ministerial decree, school teachers can provide most or even all the training. But the new breed of 'chalk-on-their-hands' educators are unlikely to go solo in large numbers just yet. We think that a re-defined partnership between schools and education departments is the best way forward. We also believe that this is the type of training model that you're most likely to encounter when you start your course.

The conventional roles, of tutors who dealt with reflective issues and teachers who handled the 'nuts and bolts', are merging into a partnership where campus tutors and school mentors are together focusing on providing the skills which underpin classroom practice. The classroom has wrested centre stage from the lecture hall, and the other components of teacher education courses are being press-ganged into its service. The 'ologies' are in retreat and competences are on the march.

Even the tutors are going back to school. In responding to the DfE's requirement that student teachers log more time in schools, the

University of London's Institute of Education is sending its academics into the classrooms to join them. And let's not be glib about this. These days, education tutors are not as removed from what goes on in schools as some people might think. Some of the best teachers have gone on to become university tutors. Moreover, recent and relevant classroom experience features prominently in teacher educator recruitment. This means that many of the tutors have previously worked with school students in the same age and ability range for which they're now preparing student teachers to teach. Going back to school means going back to familiar settings, even though certain aspects of the landscape may have changed.

When they're not re-acquainting themselves with the school experience, tutors are linking campus courses to what intending teachers need to know before stepping into the classroom. In the partnership teacher education scheme, to which the writers of this book belong, tutors and mentors focus on common goals. PGCE science specialists, for example, are briefed on campus about how to work in school science laboratories. Then they go to schools to watch experienced teachers supervising science practicals. Thereafter, it's time to have a go.

The 'listen-watch-do' model is an inevitable part of the new competence-driven training. Schools are also using their knowledge of the demands made on newly qualified teachers to help education departments provide instruction that is closely linked to practical application. The knowledge base of serving school teachers is thereby moving into the universities.

In our school, two mentors (one of the writers and a science teacher) are researching the means by which classroom skills become incorporated into the developing professional competences of student teachers. We initiated this research and the university have given us their backing, including the expert services of three academic staff. The research is practitioner-led and is designed to enable the school and the university systematically to identify the processes whereby class-management skills are acquired and augmented by student teachers during and even beyond pre-service training. Our aim is to enable mentors and tutors to target and provide those aspects of competences instruction which register high levels of trainee receptiveness. The mentors involved in the research are particularly interested in testing a claim by one of the tutors that the observation by student teachers of successful, experienced teachers in action gives little explicit guidance on effective lesson management because good teachers make things look too easy.

Whatever results emerge – the research is still underway – the university is encouraging 'practitioners-as-researchers' to help shape future teacher education programmes. This represents a welcome departure from the conventional view that classroom research and course development is best left to campus academics. Now that mentors and tutors address a common agenda, they're more likely than in the past to rotate their previously quite distinct roles. If other institutions follow the example of the London Institute of Education – and send their tutors back into classrooms – it might become more difficult to make a meaningful distinction between the job of a tutor and the job of a mentor.

Assessing performance

The educators of tomorrow's teachers know from their own experience that no student teacher could possibly absorb the range of relevant knowledge and acquire the necessary skills during pre-service courses to handle all the demands that the modern school places upon its staff. But you will be expected, during the dry-run phase of Initial Teacher Training, to show your instructors that you've stockpiled sufficient practical know-how to step into a classroom on day one of your first appointment and be able to handle the basics.

You will have learnt, for example, that students place a very high premium on having a teacher who explains things clearly in language they can relate to and understand. The possession of quite a reasonable degree of confidence in that competence will have been expected by your mentors and tutors and – hopefully, by you – by the time you pick up your BEd, BA/BSc(NQT), PGCE or other teaching qualification. It's likely that your progress in acquiring the ability to make the complex simple will have been monitored and logged by you and your educators in the form of a 'competence profile': a formative document which charts your encounters (successful and, invariably, at times, otherwise) with the skills in question.

The profile is a good assessment tool: it expects development, it anticipates that things will get better, it notes difficulties but it points to solutions. It's a more reliable means of systematically identifying and charting the developing craft competences of the student teacher than a 'frozen-in-its-tracks', final grade. Good profiles are focused without being absurdly atomistic; they deal with the bold outlines rather than all the constituent elements. It's more helpful and meaningful to report, for example, that, 'Following the student teacher's step-by-step instructions in clear, simple language, students who were previously unable to do this task were able to accomplish it with obvious success', than, 'On a scale of 1 to 10, the student teacher scored 8 for unambiguous language, less 2 for not smiling enough, 7 for resonant voice production, plus a bonus point for appropriate gesticulation'.

Most Initial Teacher Training institutions in the UK now use profiling. Moreover, the DfE is committed to the view that a profiling system, designed to support competence-driven courses, will help ease the transition from initial training to professional induction. In that respect, the profile carries forward the competence instruction and assessment of performance started in the pre-service training and makes it an essential feature of further professional development.

Incidentally, by the time that double-espresso type jolt to the nervous system starts to abate when you address a class of students, you'll know you're becoming a real professional.

Getting the best out of teacher education

Whatever route you decide to take into the teaching profession, it's very important that you use the expertise and facilities at your disposal during training to the full. You might never again have access to such a wide range of material and human resources as you'll find in what, for most of you, will be a university and a network of partnership schools. Tap into the expertise that is on offer. It will stand you in good stead when you start your teaching career.

Dress rehearsals

It's probable that you will be doing a course that involves both a university dimension and school-based observation and practice. In that case, the minimum time you will spend in schools is likely to be as follows:

Secondary courses
24 weeks in full-time PGCE courses
18 weeks in part-time PGCE courses
24 weeks in two and three-year undergraduate courses

32 weeks in four-year undergraduate courses.

Primary courses
18 weeks in full and part-time PGCE courses
18 weeks in two-year undergraduate courses
24 weeks in three-year undergraduate courses
32 weeks in four-year undergraduate courses.

What you do in university will be, in large part, a dress rehearsal for these substantial school-based components. Undergraduate courses will involve more directed time on subject knowledge and subject application studies than postgraduate courses. But there will still be a prominent focus in postgraduate courses on the application of student teachers' subject specialisms to the teaching and assessment of school students.

Whatever time you spend on subject knowledge studies – and this is clearly related to whether you embark on undergraduate, postgraduate or special one year courses – your training will place a high priority on subject application, that is, on teaching your subject in a way that enables your students to understand and enjoy what's going on. On campus, you'll be taught by tutors who should know a thing or two about effective instructional styles. After all, they are experts in the field. Study the best ones at their craft in the lecture hall, in the seminar room, or wherever they display their professional competencies.

Some will excel in the traditional didactic manner: standing at the lectern and dazzling the audience with an array of eloquently turned phrases, audio-visual displays that connect with monitors at precisely the right moment without the distraction of technical hitches, hard-hitting statements and unbridled polemic that challenge those who dare to remain complacent, with invitations towards the end for rebuttals and counter-claims. These lectures will be short, explosive, thought-provoking, and probably controversial. They'll have been prepared with meticulous precision, right down to dry-run practices in front of an imaginary audience, and the props will have been tested and re-tested before and on the day of the real event. Content will have been thoroughly researched, and difficult issues will be presented in language that simplifies and entertains simultaneously.

Note the teaching techniques that impress you in the lecture-hall and apply them in the classroom. Concise, punchy lectures are excellent ways to get school students interested in new topics. Begin them with a 'whet the appetite' starter, for example, 'Robin Hood – fact or fiction? Let's consider the real evidence'. Then follow up with a short (about twenty minutes) lecture. Include clips from various Robin Hood films (copyright permitting), and temper the Hollywood versions with simplified accounts of actual debates between historians on the authenticity or otherwise of the Robin Hood legend. Invite students to respond to your lecture, either by asking you questions or by making their own comments.

Learn, too, from the tutors who excel in the more interactive setting of the seminar – often conducted in a workshop fashion. Seminars dispense with the sartorial gravitas of the lecture and are altogether much more informal affairs. Good seminars enlarge knowledge bases and extend critical faculties with a minimum of 'teacher talk'. They force students to take a direct role in their own learning. Tutors ask questions, encourage independent thinking, and provide guidance rather than answers. There is more tutor involvement, though, than meets the eye. Effective tutors create and sustain an active learning environment of props, cues and other stimulus material. They produce an agenda of sorts, but they make students feel in control of what happens thereafter. They know that a minimum of 'teacher talk' doesn't mean a maximum of whimsical diversions and they work just as hard in the seminar room – perhaps harder – as in the lecture hall.

Seminar-style instruction also works well in the classroom. Once you've introduced a new topic with an engaging lecture, a discussion provides an excellent follow-through activity. You're unlikely to enjoy the small group sizes which university tutors work with, but you can always split a large class into smaller units. More about that and about whole-class teaching in Chapter 4, which deals with class management.

Meanwhile, remember that the 'tutor as maestro', addressing seat rows of students, and the 'tutor as coach', orchestrating group-based learning tasks, are not alternative options. The counterparts of these models in the school setting, 'maestro' whole-class teaching and 'coach' group-directed work, should both be used because good teaching involves diversity. You'll experience this diversity in the training you receive on campus. Learn from the best of your tutors, savour their great moments, and deploy some of their magic when you teach.

The real thing

It is almost certain that you'll be given the opportunity to watch experienced teachers in action before you take the plunge yourself. Ask to shadow one of them for a day or two. That way, you'll get more insights into their work than if you keep to the more usual pattern of watching set-piece teaching, carefully orchestrated pastoral activities, and pre-planned responses for dealing with students who are known to 'play up'. Become a fly on the wall at staff meetings, watch how teachers deal with incidents in school canteens and corridors, venture in to playgrounds and on to sports fields. Get a feel of the school: its atmosphere, its ethos, its temperament. Look for the authentic, not the sanitised.

Knowing your way around the unstated agenda of a school, its hidden curriculum, is just as important as being aware of its more explicitly stated up-front messages. Once you've tuned into the culture of a school, you'll be better able to fit your own aspirations into a realistic framework when it's time to do some teaching yourself. You might prefer to have students call you by your first name, but, if they're instructed to address teachers as Ms Hemingway, Sir, Miss etc., you're asking for trouble. The quickest way to court disaster in a school that insists on being formal, is to embark on a Summerhillean, call me Tony, quest for progressive enlightenment.

The system is more powerful than you. Some students might appreciate your obvious friendliness, but others will see you as a 'pushover'. We are sorry to talk in these terms because we are very idealistic and progressive ourselves. But we have learnt that being called 'Sir' needn't represent capitulation to the ideals we hold dear: making our lessons fun, getting our students through examinations (it does make a difference to their futures), treating them with courtesy, and showing them that we care. If you prefer to work in an informal educational setting, find a school where being addressed as 'Miss' or 'Sir' is as equally iconoclastic as being called by your first name in a more formal context. Such schools exist. I have worked in them and I feel more at home in them. But, for the time being, apart from inviting older students to call me by my first name on school outings (there are few takers), I settle for 'Sir'.

If possible, try out different types of institution during the school-based parts of your training. It's helpful to spend some time in schools where the institutional cultures support different norms: schools with and without uniforms, schools where 'Miss' and 'Sir' are how students address teachers and schools where everybody is on first name terms, schools which believe in 'back to basics', and schools where a student-centred learning ethos prevails. Cut your teeth on the tough inner-city school, as well as the one in the leafy suburb. Perhaps you can do a main teaching placement in one institution and an observation period in another.

You will probably find the kind of school that suits your temperament and your values if you pick and mix during these school-based cycles. If you do, tell the teachers to whom you are attached, and the senior staff, that this is the type of school where you would like to work, and that you would welcome the opportunity to apply for any posts that might arise.

School cultures aside, your placements will give you valuable opportunities to engage in real teaching. When you watch skilful practice, you gain privileged access to the accumulated professional skills of experienced teachers. Try to incorporate some of their strategies into your own teaching. What better way to take a shortcut than to imitate the things that work, the things that experienced teachers have found make them better at their profession? Find good role models during your on-the-job-training, observe them with intent, identify and note their star qualities, video them with a camcorder and watch the replays, and, within the authentic schema of your own attributes and personality, put what you admire into practice.

At the same time, be aware that the competence-based expertise of professional teachers is not reducible to a bag of tricks. As Ted Wragg (1993) correctly notes: 'Professional competence is intelligent thought translated into intelligent action'. How you apply your newly acquired skills, involves well-informed assessments of the contexts – cognitive, emotional, gendered and other – upon which intelligent (and principled) practice must be premised.

Not just a bag of tricks

Although the DfE is placing considerable emphasis on picking up the 'tricks of the trade' during Initial Teacher Training, this can never be the full story. Learning to teach must mean more than the acquisition of practical coping strategies. Dealing with a student, who refuses to do what a teacher says, cannot adequately be handled by invoking a formulaic class-management procedure. Perhaps there is a psychological or social dimension to the refusal that requires a more imaginative response from the teacher than the application of an off the peg solution. I remember protesting to a deputy head – during an interview for a teaching post – that I could not conjure up a stock retort when a school student (role-played by the deputy) refused to get on with her work when instructed to do so. 'I'd need to be there', I said, 'to get a feel of the situation, to know more about this student, finding out what happened to her this morning before she came to school.'

As a teacher, you need to develop a sensitivity for understanding the contexts in which human behaviour – rebelling, learning, crying, shouting, smiling, achieving – take place. There is a place for critical reflection, for the study of philosophy, psychology and sociology in Initial Teacher Training. Opting for a discovery approach in one lesson, a 'pump-in-some-facts' approach on another occasion, calls for an awareness of wider issues.

Take, for example, classroom work on prejudice and discrimination. In a class of predominantly white students containing one black student, is it appropriate to select a teaching strategy for this topic without having conferred beforehand – and in private – with the solitary black student? Is it morally justifiable to exclude the prior involvement of this student in the preparation of a lesson whose content and presentational style could, if handled insensitively, cause considerable embarrassment and hurt? Are you sufficiently aware of black issues, of the extent to which teachers can properly be involved in shaping the values of students, to be able to make the right decisions here?

Your training clearly needs to provide you with opportunities to consider, discuss and form opinions about issues like: equal opportunities, ethics, counselling, individual and social psychology, and citizenship studies. Your profession calls for you to be more than a competent instructor. It asks you to base your professional judgements on fairness, integrity and truth, as well as on the more practical demands of the classroom. Sadly, the immediacy of classroom life does not always allow sufficient time for contemplative activity. So seize the challenge, while you're at university, to rise above the mundane and the routine, to go beyond ABC and 123, to think and debate critically, and to become a reflective practitioner.

CHAPTER 2

Knowing
your subject

Chances are you'll choose to teach a subject that you found interesting
and did well at during your schooldays, or perhaps later at university.
Wise decision! Could you imagine anything worse than to teach a subject that you always found deadly dull and in which you regularly
under-achieved?

Don't be frightened to tell your students what an exciting subject
you'll be teaching them. Your enthusiasm might kindle theirs. And if
they become enthusiastic about a subject, it's likely that they'll do better in it as far as achievement outcomes are concerned than if they're
bored to tears.

A couple of years ago, one of my A Level Sociology students came
up to me on the last day of her course and told me that my students
were fortunate to have a teacher who loved his subject and wasn't
ashamed to let it show. 'That excitement which you feel for sociology,'
she said, 'rubs off on us'.

It's not often that I've received such direct compliments, but it made me resolve more than ever to keep on trying to generate the same kind of enthusiasm from my future students.

Students also admire and respect a teacher whose subject knowledge catches them unawares and kindles their curiosity:

> Did you know that scientists have recently discovered that planet Earth has a crater 185 miles wide and 15 miles deep, a huge hole the size of Belgium? It's in Mexico and it's been there for 65 million years. It was caused by an asteroid or a comet. The hole is a solar system record. It beats the previous holder of the solar system crater championship, the planet Venus. You didn't know about this? Do you want to know more?

Teachers, who are surefooted when it comes to answering questions are rated highly too. Your classroom credibility will soar if you become accomplished in that art. You will also be giving your students knowledge they are likely to remember because their questions will often be prompted by an inquisitiveness that yields maximum attentiveness when you give them the answer.

Your stature will be further buoyed up if you inject some humour into lessons:

> What do we know about this guy, Sir Isaac Newton, apart from the fact that a red delicious fell on his bonce, and that – don't you just love him for this – he invented calculus?

On a more serious but no less significant note, do not underestimate the importance of knowing the subject knowledge of the courses you will be teaching. A candidate for an A Level teaching post at our school, who struggled to answer a relatively basic question on course content, wrecked his chances of landing the job. Even if you have a Master's degree in Aeronautical Engineering, make sure that you have found out before your interview (better still, before you fill in your application) whether or not you know the GCSE Craft, Design and Technology syllabus the school teaches. Then check your knowledge carefully against its content and fill in any glaring gaps. Heed too what recent research (Wragg, 1993) has shown: 'Teachers whose subject knowledge lacks secure foundations, are likely to suffer stress.'

The DfE takes the issue of teachers' subject knowledge very seriously. Subject specialists are increasingly needed to meet the statutory obligation that all state schools have to teach the National Curriculum.

Even primary schools, where traditionally more emphasis has been placed on breadth rather than depth, on renaissance rather than specialist knowledge, are eager to recruit 'expert' teachers who can teach their own subjects to several classes and across different ages. This development is being strongly supported by the DfE. In fact, the Government recently declared that all Initial Teacher Training (primary and secondary) should make subject knowledge an integral part of the courses.

In that context, subject knowledge was designated by the DfE, in June 1992, as a Competence expected of newly qualified secondary school teachers. One year later, in June 1993, the DfE announced that this directive (in slightly modified form) would apply to intending primary school teachers.

Let us now look at the subject knowledge criteria that underpin that Competence, as far as the educating of future secondary school teachers is concerned.

Under Section 2.2 of the DfE Initial Teacher Training (Secondary Phase) Circular 9/92:

Newly qualified teachers should be able to demonstrate:

2.2.1 an understanding of the knowledge, concepts and skills of their specialist subjects and of the place of these subjects in the school curriculum

2.2.2 knowledge and understanding of the National Curriculum and attainment targets (NCATs) and the programmes of study (PoS) in the subjects they are preparing to teach, together with an understanding of the framework of the statutory requirements

2.2.3 a breadth and depth of subject knowledge extending beyond PoS and examination syllabuses in school.

Official documents can easily make the familiar in life strange. We'll de-mystify things with a much more concise and simple translation of the above Competence: 'Be well-informed about your subject, and know how it fits into the school curriculum'. And there you have it!

The school curriculum is largely defined by the National Curriculum, Religious Education and public examinations. Depending on your specialist subject, you will be involved in one or more of these elements.

Intending teachers of students aged up to 18, should know their specialist subject at degree or equivalent level. But if you also wish to teach a second subject to students up to age 16, you should have at least A Level or comparable knowledge in that subject, supplemented by further study during Initial Teacher Training (Council for the Accreditation of Teacher Education, 1992).

So, that's it! Well, not quite perhaps. What are these NCATs and PoS things? We had to tag 'things' on the end there because the plural of PoS sounds a bit like the townsfolk in Wild West movies who get deputised to bring in bank robbers. Come to think of it, our deputies at school sometimes have to send out posses to round up wayward students.

We'll take a closer look at NCATs, PoS things and other mysteries of the National Curriculum in a section that shortly follows, called, *Making sense of the National Curriculum*. When you've read that section, you'll have made some serious headway in fulfilling DfE Competence 2.2.2 !

First, though, it needs to be emphasised that the National Curriculum is not the only 'syllabus' taught in schools.

Teaching outside the National Curriculum

The Statutory Curriculum (also called the Basic Curriculum) comprises ten National Curriculum subjects plus Religious Knowledge. The ten subjects are: English, Mathematics and Science (so-called core subjects), and Art, Geography, History, a Modern Foreign Language, Music, Physical Education, and Technology (including IT). Welsh is a core subject in Wales where Welsh is the main medium of instruction. However, the publication on 5 January 1994 of an important report on the National Curriculum by Sir Ron Dearing (Chair of the School Curriculum and Assessment Authority) heralded the implementation, from September 1995, of a much less prescriptive Basic Curriculum. More about this in the next section. Meanwhile, if your specialist subject is not on the Basic Curriculum menu, worry not: there is still an important role for you to play. Moreover, things are looking better these days for teachers of optional subjects like Business Studies, Law, Psychology, Sociology, and a whole range of vocational subjects, especially if their subject knowledge enables them to teach students in the 16–19 age range.

These subjects are 'crowd-pullers' in the post compulsory curriculum.

The candidature nationally for A Level Sociology, for example, was second only to A Level English in 1993. Moreover, further education and sixth form colleges are currently witnessing a massive surge in the numbers of students signing up for A Level Psychology. Social Science teachers are also increasingly called upon to provide expert input into the increasingly popular General National Vocational Qualification: more about GNVQs later.

So, hopefully for you specialists, whose subjects don't form part of the Basic Curriculum, more teacher education courses in your field could be set to come on stream. Bearing in mind also that Year 12, 13, and 14 students (the modern description for 'sixth formers') generate about £2500 per head each year to state school coffers, teachers of social sciences and vocational subjects are increasingly seen as providers of additional finance, as well as popular courses.

Teachers whose expertise lies outside the Basic Curriculum, will also be encouraged to know that Sir Ron's decision to provide a slimmer, less tightly prescriptive National Curriculum, with some of the present content becoming optional, will release time for the teaching of:

- non-statutory material in the programmes of study for National Curriculum subjects; teachers of GNVQ courses in Business and Finance, for example, could find themselves stretching the 'beyond core skills' of budding mathematicians
- more subjects not included in the National Curriculum to students up to age 16, for example, Classics and Economics. Such subjects have sometimes been 'muscled out' by the timetable arrangements of the statutory subjects. They're now staging a come-back.

It's what to do with Key Stage 4 (the 14–16 age range) which poses the most challenging and inventive way forward. Sir Ron's 'Operation Meltdown' approach has opened the door to a radical re-think on the appropriateness, in its envisaged form, of the Key Stage 4 statutory curriculum. From September 1995, the statutory curriculum at this Stage will be pruned back to:

- full courses in English, Mathematics and Science
- short courses in a Modern Language and Technology
- careers guidance, Religious and Sex Education.

History, Geography, Art and Music will become voluntary subjects for students beyond the age of 14.

This reform will open the door to a 14–19 age group continuum, encompassing craft, vocational and academic courses; and more jobs for subject specialists with knowledge that reaches beyond the compulsory curriculum.

Sir Ron isn't far away from revoking National Curriculum requirements, other than the slim-downed version described above, after age 14, and thereafter using public examination results as the main means of national assessment. What those public examinations might turn out to be also remains to be seen. If Sir Ron (or his eventual successor) heeds the recommendations of the Secondary Heads Association, GCSEs and A Levels might eventually be scrapped.

This influential organisation wants to replace these two-year courses with a series of shorter courses that would be offered at four levels: foundation, general (equivalent to GCSE and its vocational alternative), intermediate, and advanced (equivalent to A Level and its vocational alternative). The envisaged new system would be supervised by one body instead of the myriad examination boards that exist at present. Students would take modules (stage by stage units of study) instead of end of course, final examinations. The modules would be taken at levels appropriate to ability rather than at specific ages.

At the first two levels, English, Mathematics and Science would be studied for two years. Modules of Religious Education, Careers, Work Experience, Information Technology, and Personal, Social and Health Education would be taken at some time during the same two-year period. Students would also have to take at least one module each of Arts, Technology, Foreign Languages, Humanities, and Physical Education. This arrangement would leave time available for additional modules in Science, Classics or Vocational Studies. At the higher levels, students would be able to study a combination of theory-based modules in up to five different subjects and up to eight applied modules. All students over 14-years old would be taught six core skills: Communication, Numeracy, Problem Solving, Personal Skills, Information Technology, and competence in a Modern Foreign Language, either as integral parts of the curriculum or through additional studies. There would be four grades for each module: distinction, merit, pass and fail.

Whether or not this new system or something like it comes to fruition, the days of GCSEs and A Levels, at least in their present shape, could be numbered. 'Breadth rather than depth', is the rallying cry of the headteachers and other influential educationists who are calling for greater diversity in the school curriculum. However, we must not speculate too much. GCSEs and A Levels are still with us, but their scope and provisions are under review, and some changes are inevitable.

You may recall that you will need to know your main subject to degree level if you teach students up to 18-years old. We hope it is clear to you by now that, even allowing for the increasing opportunities to teach non-statutory subjects like Classics and Social Sciences to students aged 14–16, much of the teaching time allotted to specialists whose expertise lies outside the prescribed curriculum, will be with older students. The Social Sciences Department in our school, for example, offers A Levels in Law, Psychology and Sociology; there are four teachers, three of whom teach exclusively to 16–19-year-old students.

So what does this imply for the beginning teacher of a subject 'beyond the pale'? We'd say plenty of rejoicing: you're likely to be working with highly motivated students who have chosen to do your subject. They'll rightly expect you to possess high-powered subject expertise; their futures could depend on it.

The post-compulsory curriculum

Whether you're a teacher of a National Curriculum subject, Religious Education, or of a subject other than those, when you teach students aged 16 and above, you enter the post-compulsory curriculum. So what follows is not restricted to psychology teachers and the like; teachers of A Levels Mathematics, English and Sciences and any other Basic Curriculum subjects are also included.

The majority of students who choose to stay on at school after 11 years of compulsory education, either study so-called academic subjects or enter vocational courses. The academic/vocational divide is deeply rooted in the English educational psyche. It can be detected in the nineteenth-century assumption that 'gentlemen', but not 'lesser' men or women in general, only turned their hands to practical matters when engaged in war or when duels were deemed necessary to advance their reputations.

Old habits die hard in this country, and there's still a tendency among some teachers to regard vocational courses as offering low-level, non-prestigious skills to low-motivated, low-attaining students. By contrast, A Levels, those 'gold standard' benchmarks of pre-university scholarship, are ostensibly only suitable for the educational elite.

However, this quintessentially English view that students can be divided into the either/or categories of 'hands' who toil and 'heads' who think, is outmoded and educationally short-sighted. In a submission to Sir Ron (reported in *The Times Educational Supplement*, 9 July 1992), the Confederation of British Industry concluded that : 'It must become the norm for all young people to achieve valued qualifications and not just the academic few'. The Confederation also supported core skills for everyone, and the integration of the National Curriculum with National Vocational Qualifications (NVQs), GNVQs, and A and AS Levels.

The integrative model is premised on the (in our view, correct) assumption that all kinds of knowledge are worthy of celebration. In that respect, there's no inherent superiority of one course over another. Better to go for a 'pick and mix' approach to the curriculum menu than to vie one knowledge track against another.

As we write this book, we sense that there's a gently gathering momentum behind the integrationist 'cause'. At the same time, we recognise that the journey to that destination might take any number of different routes. It may be necessary to wage more concerted war on the supremacist notion that vocational courses are 'second choice' options before headway can be made in persuading teachers, students and parents that the best way forward is in the form of integrated packages. Bluntly speaking, vocational courses might have to prove their worth on the two-track highway before they can merge into one broad lane.

Signs are that's starting to happen. A number of 16-year-old students are currently turning their backs on the traditional academic A Level courses, in favour of a path leading to a new qualification: the so-called 'Vocational A Level', or, to use its proper title, the GNVQ Advanced.

This examination was piloted among 8000 students in schools and colleges in 1992, and was launched nation-wide in September 1993. Of the piloted students, half were judged to be good academic A Level material, each with at least five Grade A-C GCSEs. The startling popularity of the GNVQ Advanced is evidenced by the fact that in many

34

of the schools and colleges involved in the pilot scheme, including a Government 'flagship' City Technology College, all the students decided to opt out of conventional A Levels in favour of the new course.

Moreover, a nation-wide survey, conducted by the Universities and Colleges Admissions Service, and reported in *The Times Higher Education Supplement*, 18 February 1994, found that the GNVQ Advanced has been accepted by most colleges and universities as an entry qualification into higher education. The only courses that are not taking candidates with this qualification are those requiring specialist knowledge, such as Dentistry and Medicine.

On a cautionary note though, Professor Alan Smithers, Head of Manchester University's Centre of Education and Economic Research, has warned that the GNVQ Advanced is geared to what students can do rather than what they know. The suggestion here is that the knowledge which underpins vocational skills is inferred rather than rigorously tested. Professor Smithers's view has prompted vigorous rebuttals from defenders of the new vocational courses. At this stage, however, until more piloting is conducted, the jury is still out.

Meanwhile, it's important and necessary to persuade parents, students, teachers and university admissions tutors that vocational knowledge should be judged on its own merits. Unfortunately, our long standing attachment to the original A Level 'gold standard', still makes us think in terms of bogus equivalents. Thus GNVQ Advanced is supposedly the same as two academic A Levels. However, the sooner we adopt the more continental view that excellence comes in many forms, the sooner we'll be able to stop worrying about dubiously contrived alignments between academic A Levels and other courses.

Where does this leave you, the teacher of the post-compulsory curriculum? Despite the obvious growth in the popularity of vocational subjects, it's unlikely that most 16-year-old students will be signing up for vocational alternatives to A Levels in the immediate future. The bulk of your teaching is probably going to be with conventional A Level students, but it's very possible that your subject knowledge will be called upon to service key components of vocational courses. One of our colleagues, for example, teaches A Level Law for most of the time, but he's summoned (excuse the pun) to teach two double periods (2 x 70 minutes) weekly of Business Law to students on a GNVQ Advanced Business Studies and Finance course. It will stand you in good stead, job-wise, if you become acquainted and, if possible, involved with the new vocational courses during your school-based training. Lots of these courses are now on stream, so you'll enhance the pulling-power of your resumé by getting in some vocational teaching.

If you do teach on vocational courses, a good investment to make during pre-service or in-service training courses is to book plenty of computer time. Otherwise you'll end up like me, having to go cap in hand to the GNVQ suite, asking the students there to teach you how to handle the latest bit of software savoir-faire. But then again, maybe that's not such a bad thing. It gives those students confidence in their ability to teach the teacher a thing or two; to demonstrate that they can be partners in the quest for knowledge.

Word-processing and desktop-publishing are the software skills that will likely benefit you most if you teach on vocational courses. In an environment where pens and pencils are increasingly giving way to keyboard proficiency, computer literacy will also enable you to produce handouts that look sharp. On that matter, I recently heard a government inspector expressing dismay because a student teacher was not word-processing the otherwise excellent learning materials that she had produced for her A Level students. A bit hard you might think, but it will enhance your professional edge if you learn to put some computer magic into those wall displays, course handouts, and departmental memos.

While the post-compulsory curriculum currently starts in the school year after students reach their sixteenth birthday, Sir Ron's reforms to the National Curriculum make it possible for GCSEs to become part of a broader 14–19 educational route, with more emphasis on choice than on mandate, more opportunities to select a mix of academic and vocational subjects, and more students remaining at school after age 16.

But before we get to September 1995, let us turn the spotlight on where the 14–16 curriculum is in 1994 – largely under the statutory provisions of the National Curriculum. Where appropriate, the next section will also highlight impending changes to the existing arrangements.

Making sense of the National Curriculum

Compulsory schooling has been on English statute books since 1880. Yet, for the last hundred years or so, the law had nothing to say about what students were entitled to study at school, apart from Religious Education.

Demand for a more clearly defined entitlement curriculum grew strongly over the previous few decades. A notable milestone was the speech at Ruskin College, Oxford, in 1976 by the then Labour Prime Minister, James Callaghan, in which he called for a core curriculum of basic knowledge for all school students. Prime Minister Callaghan's bid was ratified by a Conservative Government in 1988, when the *Education Reform Act* ushered in the National Curriculum.

We earlier listed the subjects that the National Curriculum says school students aged 5–16 must study. In case you've forgotten, we'll go through them again, this time in a bit more detail. Bear in mind, however, that recent modifications, detailed below, mean that, beyond age 14, students no longer have to study all the subjects. Moreover, primary school students aren't required to study a Modern Language.

The National Curriculum in England consists of three 'core' subjects – English, Mathematics and Science – and seven other 'foundation subjects': Art, Geography, History, a Modern Foreign Language, Music, Physical Education, and Technology (including IT). Welsh is a core subject in schools in Wales where Welsh is the principal language of instruction. It's a foundation subject in schools in Wales where Welsh is not the principal language of instruction. Core and foundation subjects are often, rather confusingly, collectively referred to as foundation subjects.

Primary school students (5–11-year olds) are required to take all the subjects, apart from, as mentioned above, a Modern Foreign Language. However, from September 1995, the main emphasis is on English, Mathematics and Science, and the amount of compulsory material is halved in other National Curriculum subjects.

At age 11, students enter secondary schools. From 11–14, they must study every subject. Students aged 14–16 may currently jettison Art and Music, and may choose between History and Geography or take short courses in both. From September 1995, the new slimmed down statutory curriculum (with History and Geography already installed as options), permits students to choose non-National Curriculum subjects, like Classics, Economics, Law, Psychology and Sociology – if schools have the expertise and resources to provide these courses.

From 5–16, all students are obliged (unless their parents say otherwise) to study Religious Education, which, while not actually a

National Curriculum subject, is nevertheless a compulsory element of what is taught in England and Wales. This contributes to the spiritual and moral development which the 1988 *Education Reform Act* has pledged to provide the nation's students. The Act also endorses the cultural, mental and physical development of students.

Subjects are usually introduced at the beginning of the so-called 'Key Stages', and gradually extend to every age group in the 5–16 range. It will probably be 1996 before all year groups are covered, and 2003 before the first National Curriculum 'graduates' climb the rostrum to claim their prizes.

Key Stages

Student progress is monitored continuously by teachers, and this is supplemented by summative (end of course) formal assessments at ages 7, 11, 14 and 16. These ages mark the end of four Key Stages in the eleven years of compulsory education:

	Ages
Key Stage 1	5–7
Key Stage 2	7–11
Key Stage 3	11–14
Key Stage 4	14–16

Programmes of Study

Each subject has Programmes of Study, which set out the range of understanding, knowledge and skills that students should be taught in each Key Stage. Take Key Stage 1 History, for example. The Programme of Study for students aged 5–7, prescribes that they should understand that there is a past, that they should learn and thereby know about the past, and that they should acquire the skill of measuring the past. The last skill, for example, requires the teacher of Key Stage 1 students to use local studies in order to develop a sense of chronology.

I wish 'chronology' had been a compulsory component of History when I did my teaching practice in a tough east London comprehensive school in 1975. When asked by a history teacher, a 'make my day', enforcer type, what I proposed to teach my students, I sheepishly said that I wanted to get them to reflect on what it meant to talk about a 'past'. 'Normans', came back the reply. 'Pardon?' said I. 'Teach 'em Normans', said the 'enforcer. .... 'Yes sir!, Normans it is.'

At least he didn't have to go through what a fellow student teacher – also at the same school – had to endure. 'Call me Mike', he told his students, who then proceeded to treat him as not a 'proper' teacher. More about that in Chapter 4 on class management.

Meanwhile, back to Programmes of Study. Think of them as the content or syllabus part of the National Curriculum – what has to be taught. The next term you will need to understand is 'Attainment Targets'. These are linked to the Programmes of Study.

Attainment Targets

The content of a history course is chosen on historical grounds. The Attainment Targets that define the knowledge, skills and understanding students are expected to have of this content by the end of each Key Stage, are based on educational grounds, and thus reflect the intellectual growth of the students.

There are between one and four Attainment Targets for each National Curriculum subject. The Attainment Targets describe the knowledge, skills, and understanding that students of varying abilities and maturity are expected to develop in each subject. For example, Attainment Target 4 in Science is referred to as Physical Processes. Each Science Attainment Target is composed of so-called Strands, which describe in more detail what that expectation entails. Thus, for example, Attainment Target 4, Physical Processes, is sub-divided into five Strands.

1 Electricity and magnetism.
2 Energy resources and energy transfer.
3 Forces and their effects.
4 Light and sound.
5 The Earth's place in the universe.

Strands are more explicitly developed in some subjects (for example, Mathematics and Science) than in others (for example, English).

Perplexed? Don't be; the terminology of the National Curriculum is quite extensive and it is sufficient at this stage for you to know the main features. Leave the fine-tuning to teaching practice and professional experience, and things will fall more neatly into place.

Even if your subject is a non-statutory one, it's wise to get acquainted with the 'ins and outs' of the National Curriculum. Who knows when, like me, you might have to pull a second National Curriculum subject out of the bag: in my case, history, when I don't have a full sociology timetable? You will also increase you prospects of landing a job if you can offer a statutory subject in addition to a specialist subject that's not mandatory. Posts in National Curriculum subjects outnumber those in other subjects.

It is also possible that expertise in a non-statutory subject might be called upon to service aspects of National Curriculum teaching. For example, an economics teacher might be asked to make important cross-curriculum contributions to those National Curriculum Strands of Geography which contain 'economic activities' and the 'use and misuse of natural resources'. So persevere with this section all you economists!

Now on to the next piece in the National Curriculum jigsaw puzzle: Levels of Attainment.

Levels of Attainment (See update on page viii)

Each Attainment Target is further defined in terms of different Levels of Attainment that students can achieve. In most subjects, Attainment Targets have ten levels which cover all four Key Stages. Learning in all subjects, other than Art, Music and Physical Education, is ranked in a hierarchy of ten steps. The average student is expected to attain Level 2 by the end of her or his second year at school, ascending level by level, subject by subject, to Level 6 or 7 at the age of 16. Very able students should reach Level 10 at or even before that age.

The 10-level scale is fuelling much debate in educational and government circles at present, and its future is uncertain. For the time being though, it looks set to stay at Key Stages 1–3 (Dearing, 1993). The scale works well for some skills but less so for others. For example, a Level 5 skill in subtraction can be precisely defined and tested, and applied to any age group. But what can we make of Level 5 readers? You'll find them in every age group, from high flyer 5-year olds to dispirited 14-year olds, biding their time before they leave school. Yet in language terms, the two groups are widely separated. A 14-year old is far more likely to have reading skills in a considerably wider range of contexts than a 5-year old, even though this difference might not be picked up in a standard reading test.

Sir Ron isn't yet advising the Government to scrap the 10-level scale at Key Stages 1–3, but he has decided to dispense with it at Key Stage 4. He is also likely to seek further consultation with teachers and educationists on whether to remove it altogether. It's therefore prudent not to say too much at this time about a system that might be retained, modified or replaced.

The next item for consideration, however, the Statement of Attainment, is likely to be around for many years to come.

Statements of Attainment (See update on page viii)

As things stand, each Level of Attainment in an Attainment Target is more exactly defined by what are called Statements of Attainment. Confused ? If the reply is, 'Yes, but on a higher level', you're making progress. We sense that we're testing your patience with all this jargon! Be assured, though, that things will fall into place much more readily when you start to cut your teeth on the National Curriculum at the 'chalkface'. Meanwhile, we'll make matters clearer by describing Statements of Attainment in a real context. National Curriculum Modern Foreign Languages is the context we have in mind.

Level 1 of Modern Foreign Languages Attainment Target 1 (Listening) has two Statements of Attainment. Students should be able to:

1 understand and respond to familiar utterances up to four words
2 identify individual items in a list.

So you see, the Statements of Attainment are part and parcel of the Levels of Attainment because they describe the precise objectives of these Levels.

Now on to Standard Assessment Tasks.

Standard Assessment Tasks

How do we determine at what Level of Attainment a student is performing? There are two ways of doing this in the National Curriculum: internal teacher assessment and external examiner assessment. In both cases, students' Levels of Attainment are measured by how well they do in nationally set tasks and tests, which are collectively referred to as Standard Assessment Tasks.

Teacher assessments refer to on-site administering and marking of National Curriculum tests by the teachers, who then graduate their students' performances in line with appropriate Levels of Attainment. It is usual for peer group moderation, that is, teachers checking each other's ratings, to feature in this type of assessment.

41

The national tests are both set and marked by external examiners and are currently restricted to the three core subjects. At some point, the tests might be extended to other National Curriculum subjects but no firm decision has yet been reached on this matter. According to Sir Ron, the tests provide a valuable means of nation-wide moderation of teacher assessments, as well as giving reliable information linked to a national standard. Sir Ron is, at the same time, keen to involve teachers in regular, critical reviews of the tests. He also believes that national test and teacher assessment ratings should be indicated separately in all forms of reporting and in school prospectuses.

While the national tests and the teacher assessments form the basis for evaluating progress in Key Stages 1–3, the principal form of assessment at the end of Key Stage 4 is GCSE or equivalent examinations. From 1994, the GCSE covers National Curriculum Levels 4–10, but GCSE results are reported in letter grades. The table below shows how these letter grades correspond to Levels 4–10 (though the Levels are not reported on GCSE certificates).

GCSE letter grades	*National Curriculum Levels 4–10*
A*	10
A	9
B	8
C	
	7
D	
	6
E	
F	5
G	4

In an important sense, the GCSE has been absorbed into the assessment procedures of the National Curriculum, as demonstrated by the table. However, Sir Ron made it clear, in December 1993, that he does not think we need the 10-level scale for the majority of Key Stage 4 students. Instead, he wants to dispense with the scale at Key Stage 4, but, as indicated above, still retain the GCSE letter grades.

We'll conclude this section on the National Curriculum by providing you with an up-to-date summary of how Sir Ron's Final Report will affect you, the intending, or practising teacher.

The Government has accepted, in full, Sir Ron's main recommendations. This means that, from the 1995–6 school year, it will introduce a streamlined curriculum, giving much more scope to teacher discretion, while also retaining the key provisions of the current National Curriculum. The most important reforms are:

- slimming down the mandatory curriculum for 5–14-year-old students, particularly outside the core of English, Mathematics and Science, thereby releasing an average of 20 per cent of time for schools to use at their own discretion
- reducing the number of Attainment Targets to 25, compared to the previous 36. This makes record-keeping and reporting simpler. Teachers are to judge at the end of each Key Stage how well students have performed on the basis of broader Statements of Attainment, known as Level Descriptions. These are calibrated over 10 Levels of Attainment, but cover only students aged 5–14, compared to the previous 5–16-year age-range
- providing more scope, from 1996–7 onwards, for 14–16-year-old students to study academic options and to select from a wider range of vocational courses. From 1996, the mandatory curriculum for students in this age group will be confined to: full courses in English, Mathematics and Science; short courses in Technology and a Modern Foreign Language; PE; Religious Education; and Sex Education
- changing the 10-level scale to reduce significantly the number of criteria – 'Statements of Attainment' – that define what students must be able to do at each Level.

The new curriculum requirements are scheduled to be settled by the end of 1994, and schools are due to receive the new curriculum in January 1995. Following the implementation of the new curriculum for students aged 5–14 in September 1995, Sir Ron wants no major changes for five years, which will be a major relief to most teachers.

Meanwhile, it's important to realise that Sir Ron's Final Report leaves these curriculum features the same:

- the range of subjects for 5–14-year-old students remains unchanged
- in each of those subjects, the streamlining process will retain intact an unchanged core of mandatory content
- teachers are at liberty to continue teaching aspects of the curriculum that have become voluntary
- tests will continue to focus on basic literacy and numeracy for 7-year-old students, and on English, Mathematics and Science for 11 and 14-year-old students
- the current A*–G Grade scale for GCSE examinations is to be kept.

We hope, by now, that you've absorbed the broad outlines of this section on the National Curriculum, and thereby increased your awareness of a DfE Competence.

But what does the DfE expect of you when it says that you need to have, 'a breadth and depth of subject knowledge extending beyond PoS and examination syllabuses in school'? By reading the next section, you'll find out.

Beyond ABC and 123

These days, whether you're teaching Key Stage 3 Geography, A Level Music, or GNVQ Intermediate Health and Social Care, the DfE, as reported in sub-clause 2.2.3 of the Subject Knowledge Competence, expects you to go beyond the mere content knowledge of Programmes of Study and examination syllabuses. If you also look again at sub-clause 2.2.1 of the same Competence, you'll note, too, that newly qualified teachers are expected to understand the concepts and skills of their subject.

Put simply, you will need to ensure that on top of facts, you can also interpret material, analyse data, weigh up arguments, and – where appropriate – display adroitness in practical and technical matters. Definite musts in that last context, are the ability to handle basic computing operations (especially, word-processing and data-base retrieval), and simple audio – visual equipment. Make sure, therefore, that you take every opportunity during your training to gain hands-on experience in these areas.

You might think that, as a subject specialist, you're already strong on concepts. But guard against complacency. Twist your subject inside out, turn it over, and re-evaluate its central tenets. Remember those teachers who inspired you. They did not have all the answers; they encouraged you to take risks with your thoughts and ideas, to look beyond the obvious answer, to challenge uncritical acceptance of text-book surety and comfortable truths. By looking anew at your subject from a critical perspective, you will invigorate your intellect and develop the right sense of mischief to rebut the taken-for granted view of familiar texts. The rub-off effect on your students, will be to get them to think rather than to rely too much on made-to-measure rote.

It's so easy to depend on what the conventional textbooks say about particular parts of a syllabus, without probing further and discovering alternative and possibly better interpretations. I remember getting rather irritated by a familiar practice in sociology textbooks of trundling out an allegedly outdated theory and its principal advocate, before banishing both with pretty rough justice. When I looked more deeply into things, taking time to ponder issues that rarely appeared in the usual sources, I found that important aspects of the purportedly defunct theory and its author were outstandingly perceptive and very relevant to current thinking. I've passed on this finding to my students, using language and explanations they can relate to and understand, and I've simultaneously helped them to write more critically – which will earn them more marks in public examinations.

We realise, of course, that there are certain basics in most – if not all subjects – which, at school level, have to be taught as givens. But make sure that the givens are just that, rather than issues which might be contested. There are times when we need to tell students that some conclusions are better than others, that two and two are four, not five, that smoking increases the risk of lung cancer, even though Uncle Billy smoked three packets a day and lived to be a hundred. Conversely, it would be wrong to teach, for instance, that there's only one correct accent in a language, or that the accounts of generals are more worthy of historical consideration than the memories of front-line troops.

So make a distinction in your own mind and in the minds of your students between the incontestables and the contestables in the subject you teach. You don't have to wait until undergraduate level before doing this, even if some of your previous teachers didn't invite you to be discerning.

You'll also find that the invigorating debates and discussions that transcend the sometimes limiting parameters of content-based syllabuses, will better enable your students to add spark and style in National Curriculum tests and public examinations. Indeed, there are encouraging signs that examining boards today are more likely than previously to allocate fixed percentage marks to skills such as being able to distinguish between facts and values, between evidence and conjecture. Rightly, students will still earn marks for recall and effective communication of content knowledge. But the 'write all I know' approach isn't likely to gain top scores.

To some extent, your subject will influence the balance between certitude and debate in lessons. In that respect, it is true that mathematics, science and technology are more likely to emphasise factual understanding than are English, history and art. But this divide is not always clear-cut. There are still histories that don't get much beyond the chronicles of 'great men', presented as definitive accounts, just as there are technologies which encourage polemic and reflection. No subject should insist that its discourse is confined to exclusively right or wrong solutions.

Moreover, don't dodge challenges to prevailing orthodoxies by insisting that teachers always know best. That's no way to encourage the spirit of inquiry and discovery upon which new knowledge is premised. By becoming more familiar with the conceptual and philosophical elements of your subject, you'll be better placed to inject some healthy scepticism into your lessons. We want our students to know that they can dissent with great intensity from our views, provided that their arguments do not offend or hurt.

There are few things more dispiriting than working with a class who are content to let the teacher remain the jug filling the mugs. Just picture that kind of class: sitting there assiduously jotting down dictated notes and chalkboard script, waiting for somebody else to take the initiative, fearful lest their ideas will provoke a put-down from the teacher. Get into that classroom and stir things up: 'Some people claim that what's written on a London bus ticket is just as interesting as a play by Shakespeare. What do you say to that Joanne?' Or what about: 'Social scientists argue that people are much more likely to be poor because of low wages than by being lazy – comments please.'

Teachers are much more ready these days than before to support the spirited defence of an idea, even if it doesn't necessarily accord with their own views. Our previous headteacher proclaimed loudly and clearly in the school prospectus that, 'no-one is right by right and ... everyone and everything can be challenged provided that the challenge be made openly and courteously'.

Students sometimes seem perplexed by the idea that their voice has a right to be heard, to be allowed to contest a time-honoured account, to be confident in suggesting to a teacher that maybe the answer that the syllabus seems to want might not be the best answer. If you want your students to pass their examinations, getting them to access and play-back a syllabus content might do the trick. But if you want them to do better than well, encourage them to think, dare them to question, and let them know that it is safe to do these things in your lessons.

When you look beyond examination syllabuses and Programmes of Study, remember too, that in some textbooks, certain groups in society are not always presented in ways that honour their dignity and promote their well-being. Are there still books on the shelf that refer to the third person singular as masculine even when gender is not attributed by a given context: 'The scientist tests hypotheses against empirical evidence before he accepts them as facts'? Are there still posters on classroom walls that intimate that greatness is white and submission black? Scrutinise the unstated agenda of the school, its hidden curriculum, and see if equality of opportunity reveals itself therein.

Whatever the result of your search, the issue of equal opportunities is now officially on the DfE agenda. It is an area regarded by the compilers of the National Curriculum as integral to the planning, development and evaluation of what is taught in all schools. Moreover, the provision of equal opportunities has a key role to play in meeting the requirements of the 1988 *Education Reform Act*.

In that context, the former National Curriculum Council (now integrated into a new body, the School Assessment and Curriculum Authority), has made the following statement.

Providing equal opportunities for all pupils means:

- treating pupils as individuals with their own abilities, difficulties, attitudes, backgrounds and experiences
- challenging myths, stereotypes and misconceptions
- ensuring that equal access to the curriculum means real opportunity to benefit. (*Starting out with the National Curriculum*, 1992.)

Always strive to make what you teach, whether part of the National Curriculum, a public examination syllabus, or otherwise, accessible and enriching for all your students. It is important here to be flexible enough in your teaching style and in the tasks you set, to encourage wide participation by students of varying academic and social backgrounds – including students with Special Educational Needs. You will get as much joy, if not more, out of seeing the student who struggles but perseveres achieving a Grade C in a public examination, as you will get out of the high flyer who walks away with a Grade A.

For some students, a Statement of Special Educational Needs will specify that certain aspects of the National Curriculum should not apply to their learning needs, or that modifications are appropriate. That said, there is real scope for students at either end of the ability range to work successfully within the National Curriculum, and to do well in public examinations in all subjects. (More about Special Needs in Chapter 6.)

We emphasise all because some teachers, students and parents still believe that certain subjects are harder than others. But is it really possible to say that mathematics is more difficult than French, that music is not as demanding as art, or that geography is a soft touch?

We don't think so. It's really not far removed from saying that apples taste better than pears. But our opinion doesn't necessarily alter socially constructed perceptions of what's easy and what's hard.

The principal challenge in our profession, however, is to make our subject – whatever it is – easy to the students we teach, something they can understand, something they can do well in. A recently published study carried out by researchers at Bristol University and the University of the West of England (*Independent on Sunday*, 12 September 1993) found that primary school students generally liked subjects they found easy or interesting. One of the children told the researchers: 'If I don't like it I might get it wrong and then I won't like it. She gives us writing to do and it's really hard.'

We've little doubt that older students would say that the subjects they like (and do well in) are the ones which they can handle. This does not mean that teachers should spoon-feed students with material that fails to stir the imagination or which short-changes on problem-solving and discovery tasks. But it does mean that teachers should equip their students with the knowledge and skills that inspire confidence and the feeling of impending success. Being an effective teacher involves creating a learning environment in which all students make progress, whatever their original starting point. That's where subject application plays a pivotal role, and that's the topic of the next chapter.

What your mentor should do for you

There are no specific ways in which to observe subject knowledge, except in its application. So turn to the *What your mentor should do for you* section of Chapter 3, *Teaching your subject*, for guidelines on the observation of effective subject application.

Meanwhile, seek some help from your mentor in the practical areas listed below.

PRACTICE

- Ask the mentor to provide you with copies of your prospective timetable and of the syllabus(es), Programmes of Study etc., that you'll be teaching before you begin your school-based training. If possible, get hold of some of the materials you'll be using, for example, textbooks, handouts, CD ROMs and videos, and gear your subject knowledge to what you're actually going to teach. Ensure too that you're prepared for some second subject teaching.

- In your first week or so at school – which normally involves a fair bit of non-teaching, induction time – check with your mentor that your pre-school content knowledge preparation (first and second subjects) meets the requirements of the courses you'll be teaching, and make any necessary modifications and additions, as appropriate. It's also useful at this stage, to bring in some of your own personal resources (newspaper articles, video clips etc.) and give them a 'dry run' with your mentor.

- Seek permission of the mentor to attend school meetings that have a direct bearing on curriculum issues, and ask if you can get involved in the ensuing deliberations. Your ideas and suggestions could be valuable. These meetings might include items such as: discussions among subject specialists about how best to incorporate particular topics into Programmes of Study, what A Level syllabus should be followed, or how a department's expertise might feed into cross-curriculum work – how teachers, for example, of Personal and Social Education could provide support for certain modules in a GNVQ Health and Social Care course.

Action points

1 Be enthusiastic about your subject and project that enthusiasm vigorously.

2 Catch the imagination of your students by dazzling them with 'tales of the unexpected' about strange and wonderful worlds of facts and legends.

3 Make sure your subject knowledge, however impressive its accreditation, extends to the Programmes of Study and examination syllabuses you will be teaching.

4 Get acquainted with these areas during your Initial Teacher Training: computing; vocational courses (notably, GNVQs); a second teaching subject (preferably a mandatory one if your specialist subject is not part of the compulsory curriculum).

5 Become conversant with National Curriculum terminology, and apply this knowledge, as far as circumstances permit, during your school placements.

6 Take your students beyond 'textbook certainties' and 'conventional wisdoms' by inviting them to be critical of subject content.

CHAPTER 3

Teaching your subject

'Ms Rodrigues, can you slow down a bit?'
'I hate this lesson, it's so boring!'
'I love your lessons. I wish we could have you all the time!'

These are the kinds of comment your students might make about your lessons. Some of them may be for effect, some to defend a weakness they feel they have, but some may be an informed and insightful critique of your teaching style. It's important to listen to your students; after all they have received a lot of lessons in their time! Books like this are one thing, and university tutors and school mentors another, but ultimately you will be judged by your students and their educational performance. When a student says to you, 'I love this lesson!' and means it, it's one of life's great thrills.

So, you know your subject, you love your subject and shortly you have to start teaching it! We think every teacher at the start of an academic year, whether they're experienced or new to the profession,

51

wonders where to begin. You're faced with new classes, maybe new syllabuses, new government regulations, new colleagues and high expectations. Where do you start?

The DfE has made that decision for you. It requires teachers to plan, teach and assess the effectiveness of lessons, and has defined this requirement explicitly:

2.3 Newly qualified teachers should be able to:

2.3.1 produce coherent lesson plans which take account of NCATs and of the school's curriculum policies

2.3.2 ensure continuity and progression within and between classes and in subjects

2.3.3 set appropriately demanding expectations for pupils

2.3.4 employ a range of teaching strategies appropriate to the age, ability and attainment level of pupils

2.3.5 present subject content in clear language and in a stimulating manner

2.3.6 contribute to the development of pupils' language and communication skills

2.3.7 demonstrate ability to select and use appropriate resources, including Information Technology.

Putting this into more concise terms, Subject Application, as defined by the DfE, refers to: the ability to plan, co-ordinate and teach courses of learning, in an engaging, effective and appropriate manner, supported – as appropriate – by selected resources, including Information Technology. The DfE also says that, via this process, students' language and communication skills should be developed.

Let us start with the first item in the DfE Subject Application Competence: the production of coherent lesson plans.

Lesson plans

What initially appears daunting in the official DfE rubric on lesson plans, is relatively straightforward. Assuming you're teaching a National Curriculum subject, statutory regulations (known as Subject-based Orders) say what should be included in your curriculum parcels (Schemes of Work) for each Key Stage. You must always have these Orders (if they're relevant to your subject) to hand, when planning your teaching, along with any school policy documents or examination board guidelines and syllabuses, where these apply.

As a student teacher, I spent most of a summer holiday planning every single lesson for the next term, down to minutes and seconds. Laudable though this was, in intent anyway, it was a huge waste of time. The reason for this was that I had no idea about the expectations, abilities or personalities of the students I'd be teaching. Activities I thought Year 9 students would take a whole double lesson over, were completed in minutes. Year 7 students made a ten-minute fun diversion become a week's work. I was in trouble.

There's a joke that goes something like this:
Question: 'Excuse me, how do I get to London from here?'
Answer: 'Well, if I were you I wouldn't start from here.'

This illustrates the point perfectly. You can't plan to take your students from one place to another educationally, unless you know where they are now! Detailed planning is wasted if you don't know your target audience's requirements and working pace.

If this is the case, how do you go about preparing and planning to teach your chosen subject? Two old clichés worth thinking about are:

- don't re-invent the wheel
- don't run before you can walk.

No mentor will welcome a student teacher who reproduces a Scheme of Work like one already employed in a school. Similarly, no mentor will enjoy extricating a student from a disciplinary crisis because the first lesson they've given to a boisterous new class, is a free-form, small group discussion.

Your initial planning should be cautious and flexible and focus on the long term. You may have to plan individual lesson by individual lesson until you've established a teaching rhythm and a rapport with your classes. As it says in Statement 2.3.1, you need to produce 'coherent lesson plans'. You can't plan individual lessons coherently until you know what you need to have achieved with your classes over the longer term.

Long-term planning

This is the top level of planning. It's a simple list of the contents of the course, loosely blocked against terms or half-terms You may think this is just duplicating the information contained within your syllabuses or

National Curriculum Programmes of Study and decide not to bother with it. I find it useful for two reasons. The first is that it's rare that all your guidance can be found in one place, so by collecting the key points on to one clear sheet, it simplifies your more detailed planning. The second reason is that, by re-stating and representing your course material in your own way, you come to know it more securely. This plan may not take very long to do because it may only be a list of Schemes of Work against terms. However, it will give a sense of direction. (See Figure 1.)

The key to long-term planning is to know what the students are expected to have covered during the year. This will be specified somewhere, either in National Curriculum Programmes of Study (although these don't strictly specify what has to be done over a year, only over a Key Stage; but Levels of Attainment will dictate the order in which you should teach things), in Examination Board Syllabuses or school-based Schemes of Work. These levels are the bottom line. By the end of the year or Key Stage, the subject matter outlined in these documents must have been covered. If you break down the academic year into terms, and terms into weeks and lessons per class, you will see there is time, in most cases, to teach what is required of you. Hopefully, you will also have some time to spare for a little exploration and maybe some fun too. It's important not to panic at this stage, by turning your plans into too intensive a programme. Nobody learns effectively in an atmosphere of stress and hurry.

Having thoroughly examined all the appropriate documentation, and knowing what you have to cover in general, you now have to determine what parts of your subject need to be assessed, when and in what way. (See Chapter 5.) It's your primary task to equip your students to do the best they can when assessed. We all know that a poor performance in school can lead to disappointment in life, and, increasingly, both students and teachers are judged by performance. No student will thank you for poor assessment results; therefore the assessed aspects of your subject are the skeleton on which to hang the rest of your planned work.

Once you have identified the areas of your subject to be assessed, you will need to relate them in a meaningful way to the subject as a whole. Most psychologists will tell you that people find information easier to absorb and remember if it's clearly organised when they first encounter it. This sounds like common sense, but you'd be surprised

TERM BY TERM PLANNER

CLASS: 10 Ba   SUBJECT: English

PERIODS TAUGHT: 3+4 Mon   ACADEMIC YEAR: 93/94
                   7+8 Fri

1

1) Reading and study of "To Kill a Mockingbird", by Harper Lee.
See S.O.W. 8–10 weeks

2) If time, 1–2 exam comprehension tasks

2

1) Study of non-literary texts – Adverts – See S.O.W. 4-5 weeks
2) Block of oral work – to be decided

3) Study leave – 2 weeks
4) "Myself at 15" – autobiographical writing – 4 weeks – See S.O.W.
5) Exam practice – 1 week

3

1) Free assignment – negotiated to fill gaps in folder – 4 weeks
2) "Should children have to wear school uniform?"
Discursive unit – See S.O.W. – 3 weeks

3) Reading and study of "Our Day Out" – See S.O.W.– 4-5 weeks
4) Oral work based on above: 2–3 weeks

Figure 1 Term by term planner

how often teachers use phrases like, 'Don't worry, it'll fall into place later,' or 'If you don't mind, I'll keep questions to the end of the session.' Sometimes this approach is unavoidable, but, in general, it's good practice to organise your teaching in such a way that every aspect of it is understandable and relevant to the student from the beginning. This may mean having to return to complex issues more than once, but at least, on these return visits, the students will have a context in which to put the new information.

The assessment content of your subject needs to be put into purposeful order and mixed with the other non-assessed but relevant parts (that is, those parts of your subject that aren't mandatory, but help to illuminate the components which are). For example, in English, there are individual Statements of Attainment for spelling, presentation, use of punctuation, vocabulary and knowledge about language. An effective English teacher needs to teach these and to knit them together, in order to make students truly competent language users with some kind of overall style of language use. It's not enough merely to leave students with separate skill areas. To put it bluntly, teaching aimed exclusively at assessment can lead to bad teaching, giving students satisfactory examination results but little understanding.

Sadly, because of the pressure of time and the quantity of assessment, aspects of your subject that you're personally enthusiastic about, may have to go by the wayside. This might upset you, but you're only in the classroom to serve the students. Therefore you must make giving them the opportunity to perform to their best advantage in assessment situations your absolute priority.

The scheme of work

Having mapped out the long-term plan of your teaching, you need now, to break this up into smaller units. Most teachers, at this point, produce what is known as a Scheme of Work. This is a list of objectives, assessments and activities connected with one component or theme of your subject. For example, in history, a teacher may produce a list of activities to introduce a class to the use of primary sources of information. The important thing to note, is that, although at this point, a general notion of the time-scale of the scheme should be considered, you are not yet pinning the work to particular dates and times. Similarly, while you should know what objectives you want the class to carry out, you should not yet be detailing the exact activities and teaching styles. These details should be saved for the individual lesson plans.

The Scheme of Work is simply a list of activities related to a particular topic or subject area. Many departments in schools have sets of Schemes of Work that cover everything necessary to teach and assess the topic or subject. If they do, you're very lucky, but don't get complacent and abandon your planning. Schemes of Work do tell you what the contents of your lessons should be. However, they don't normally tell you how long each activity will take or necessarily which order of activities is best. This knowledge will come with experience. The contents of the Scheme of Work should be selectively transferred to your week by week plans. (One of my Schemes of Work is shown below.)

Once you have your Scheme of Work, you need to begin trying to map this on to the lessons that are available to you. Be cautious; a common error that enthusiastic teachers make is to try to pack too much into this time.

SCHEME OF WORK: YEAR 10

Unit Type: Literature component
Title: Exploring the characterisation In Harper Lee's *To Kill A Mocking Bird*

Stages

1 Introduction
a) Teacher uses Q&A to remind class of the major characters in the book, and the theme of seeing the world from other people's points of view. This could have been prepared for by a previous homework.

b) Teacher divides group up into fives, and allocates each student in a group one character from the following: Scout, Mayella Ewell, Boo Radley, Atticus Finch, Tom Robinson. If the numbers don't work out, then one of these may have to be omitted. Alternatively, if you have an excess in one group, then Mr Ewell or Calpurnia may be added to the list.

c) The members of the group are then set the task of trawling the text (probably already annotated), to find quotations and information relevant to their character's motivation and role. This may take the whole lesson and a homework.

2 Preparation and performance
a) Having collected their information, the students are instructed to rehearse in their groups, in role as their character, asking each other questions, as if they are interviewing the other characters from the book (e.g. Tom might ask Mayella whether she will be able to live happily knowing that her lies caused his death). An oral assessment may take place of this preparation. The students are urged to use voice, facial expression and body language to convey the emotions and moods of the characters.

b) Following the rehearsal, each group performs their role plays in front of the rest of the group. Optionally, the teacher may ask or allow other members of the group to ask additional un-rehearsed questions to test depth of understanding. Formal assessment of the product should take place at this time.

Alternatives and extensions

1) Instead of the set-piece interview, the students could be asked to script and perform an autobiographical monologue from the point of view of their character (e.g. I am Boo Radley).

2) The information gathered could be used as input to a traditional character study essay.

Planning for the term

For each term, for each class, you need to list the major components of the Scheme of Work against the lessons available. It's important that these plans are not too detailed because you need to be flexible at this point. That said, you can start to firm up your plans a little, as illustrated in the example provided in Figure 2 on page 59.

You need to include assessment objectives, examination dates, possible activities, marking schedules, homework, resources bookings and other important details. At this point, you must familiarise yourself with your school's academic calendar. There will be events that cut into the available time for teaching, for example, sports days or study

WEEK BY WEEK PLANNER

CLASS: 10Ba

SUBJECT: English

PERIODS TAUGHT: 3+4 Mon
7+8 Fri

TERM: 1 (Autumn)

WEEK	SESSION 1	SESSION 2
1	Intro. "To Kill a Mockingbird" Background + reading + Q and A	Show first 10 mins of video (book video room). Discussion on setting and character of "Scout" Homework - find out about America at this time
2	Read Chapters 2+3; Q and A Begin a who, when, where (3ws) chart	Cont. 3 ws chart Homework - complete chart so far
3	Read Chapters 4+5; Q and A Talk through characters	Plan and commence character studies (Deadline Week5) Homework update - 3 ws chart + character studies
4	Read Chapters 5+10; Q and A Update 3 ws chart Homework - read up to Chapter 20 + character studies	Oral work preparation The truth game - in role questioning of characters Homework - prep this
5	Cont. Collect character studies Homework - read up to Chapter 25	Oral presentations - assessed Book video camera
6	Cont. Book video camera. Homework - read up to Chapter 28	Watch 1st ½ video Book video room
7	Finish reading book Class discussion	Watch 2nd ½ video Book video room
8	Discuss and plan essay - "Mayella, Tom and Boo are all victims of Maycombe society." Discuss	Cont. Commence production Homework - cont. work

Figure 2 Week by week planner

leave, and these must be taken into account. You need to underestimate the amount you think you'll get done in your initial plan because unexpected problems may arise: fire alarms and large-scale student or staff absences are prime examples. There's always more you can add to fill in time, but, if you overload on content, you may not complete it all or you might be forced to break off at an inconvenient point.

These high level plans give you an overall view or map for each class. They then need to be broken down into more detailed views. I use sheets that cover half a term. (See Figure 2, on page 59, on which I enter, in general terms, the contents of each lesson.) While the plans may have to be adjusted as the term progresses, this does give the teacher the opportunity to book additional equipment, specialist rooms or staff, well in advance. It has the additional benefit of affording the opportunity to stagger the marking load from different classes across the term. When all classes hand in work to be marked in the same week, you will know the meaning of pressure!

Lesson by lesson

Once you have achieved this long-term and medium-term planning, it is time to get down to the lesson by lesson level. This is best done on a weekly or even day-by-day basis until you have a feel for your classes. The most important thing about lesson by lesson planning, is deciding exactly what you want your students to achieve by the end of each lesson. This is not as easy as it sounds, if you're unfamiliar with the class. Classes all have their own dynamics and pace of work. Also, these class characteristics may alter from day-to-day according to the previous lesson, the weather, the day on which the lesson falls (the last two lessons on a Friday often need a more structured approach than any other time of the week) or your own state of mind.

As we are writing this, we can imagine some teachers saying in response to it, 'You mustn't let the tail wag the dog!' Like a lot of clichés, this one has some truth in it. It's an unwise teacher who lets the whims of a group, their likes and dislikes, dictate a scheme of work or a lesson plan to her or him. It's an unwise teacher who lets worries about popularity with a class, decide the style of their teaching. That said, it's an equally unwise teacher who adheres to a lesson plan when the lesson is clearly not working. Also, you must beware of interrupting a class who are enthusiastically and productively carrying out a task, merely because the lesson plan dictates it. There are times when the dog should wag!

When you decide to go with the flow or when you choose to direct it, depends on your own teaching style, the environment in which you teach, the age of the students, whether your lesson is content or skills-based, your own personality, and, most importantly, your rapport with the students. We are sorry that more practical guidelines can't be given here but most teachers will tell you that, within an envelope of good practice, there will always be classes with whom you can do any kind of activity you like and others who will always need a rigorously imposed, structured environment. What we mean by this is that some classes are more cohesive than others. If you have a class containing many strong personalities in competing peer groups, it is more difficult to control whole group activities. You may have carefully to design small groups, recognising social tensions. Also, certain tasks will influence the selection of particular methods. For example, tasks that involve problem-solving and initiative on the part of the students cannot, by definition, be totally teacher-led, but must be highly structured and closely overseen to make sure that students remain engaged and on task. Having settled on the contents of your lesson, you now need to break the lesson up into separate chunks. The lesson plan which is shown in Figure 3, on page 62, exemplifies this point.

As you can see on this plan, a variety of activities are specified. This is for a very good reason. It's a sad fact but many teachers demand boredom thresholds and levels of concentration that they themselves could not sustain. We must always remember that we are dealing with people who may not share our enthusiasm for our subject. Without bombarding the class with a welter of activities or introducing distracting 'bells and whistles', it's vital to ensure that there is a mixture of passive, active, interactive and student-led activities. This isn't always possible but you must always remember that the attention span of even a highly motivated student is not without limits.

It's an important piece of good practice that you explain the aims and objectives of the lesson to the students at the beginning of every session. You must tell them how the lesson connects with previous ones and what you expect them to have achieved by the end of the lesson, if necessary giving chapter and verse regarding Attainment Targets or assessments. Even the most futile and onerous task can be invested with an aura of urgency and importance, if it is put into the overall context of progression through the course. There must, therefore,

LESSON PLAN

Date: 18/3/94   Class: 10 Ba
Room: 21   Time: 10.05 – 11.00

Special memos.

Remember to get Rose's book. Take in rough drafts.

Connection with previous work.

Cont. study of "To Kill a Mockingbird"

Aims To increase understanding of the motives of
        the characters
Objectives
1) To assess ATI
2) To increase understanding of text
3) To establish working groups in class

Materials/equipment

A4 paper ; 10 X tape recorders + 10 tapes

Preparations
Character studies in rough to help "stuck" students.

Contents
   1) Intro : 5 minutes
   2) Organising class into small groups : 3 minutes
   3) Oral preparation (assessed) : 45 minutes
   4) Packing up : 2 minutes

Time scale   6 - lessons

Options Groups giving class a preview of performance

Closure
        Homework – cont. preparation

Review A productive but rather noisy lesson. Perhaps
better engineering of groups would help. Too much
assistance needed — more guidance at start?

Figure 3 Lesson plan

62

always be a sense of movement and relevance in your lessons, if you want to avoid the dreaded question, 'What do we have to do this for?'

Once again, referring to the lesson plan (Figure 4), it may look a little detailed and you may wish to simplify it somewhat, but we believe that the following sections are the bare minimum.

Content

You may be surprised to see that the content of the lesson is timed down to minutes. Obviously, these timings may have to change slightly in the classroom, but it is useful to establish a structured succession of events if your teaching is to have clear rhythm. Government inspectors also expect this kind of detail in your planning.

Materials and equipment

This is also very useful, ensuring that you have everything you need for your lesson and that you don't have to resort to sending students on errands to borrow paper, books etc. or worse still, have to leave the room yourself. Leaving a class unattended should, except in cases of emergency, be avoided.

Options

Also very important. You should always specify an alternative activity here, so you can seamlessly continue, should one of your other activities fail to last the requisite amount of time. Even the most experienced teachers occasionally find they have five or ten minutes of free time at the end of a lesson, and most of them have assembled a range of games or other activities to fill this gap.

Closure

You should also specify your closure to the lesson. It's no good staggering your marking load, if, in the heat of the moment, you forget to take in the exercise books at the end of the lesson or if you forget to set homework that you're going to use as the launch pad for your next lesson with the class.

Review

It's helpful, particularly at the beginning of your teaching career, to review every lesson immediately it finishes, making sure you concentrate on things that went right, as well as on things that went wrong. A considered reflection on each lesson will give you a fund of information on which to base your future plans. It will give you a sense of progression and make personalised target setting easier. For example, if you can look back through your lesson plans and spot that every time you attempt a question and answer session with a class, it doesn't work, then clearly this is a problem area for you.

Planning: some final points

If the method of planning described above, seems to you cumbersome, or involving too much paper, you need to bear in mind that the long-term and medium-term planning only needs to be done once at the beginning of the year. It's only the daily, lesson by lesson planning which is continuous. Even this, as you become more assured, will become a once a week activity. Some teachers do away with this kind of planning altogether, but unless you have an incredibly organised mind and lifestyle, that's not advisable. Most people become forgetful when they're busy, and when you're teaching a full timetable, you're often going to be busy. Knowing you've planned well, will give you confidence in your teaching. Moreover, effective planning will help you to fulfil the next requirement expected of you by the DfE: the maintenance of continuity and progression in your teaching.

Ensuring continuity and progesssion

In DfE criterion 2.3.2, it is stated that the competent teacher needs to ensure continuity and progression within and between classes and in subjects. This criterion needs a fair bit of unpacking. We read it in the following way: by 'continuity', we construe that one lesson neatly dove-tails with the next; 'progression' implies that your lessons present an ordered hierarchy of skills or content, so that at the end of the Scheme of Work, your students are progressing at a higher level than they did at the beginning; 'within classes', we take to mean guaranteeing continuity and progression for the individual members of one particular class; 'between classes', we interpret as ensuring continuity and progression for all your separate classes; 'in subjects', we regard as ensuring that the content of lessons is equivalent for parallel classes in the same subject. For example, if you have two Year 9 science classes, they should be given equivalent content. It's possible that other people may interpret this criterion differently because of its ambiguity. However, if you've planned and annotated your plans well and have kept good records regarding individual students, no one can ask more of you than that.

Continuity within classes

On one occasion, because I had failed to annotate my lesson plans at the end of the last session with a particular Year 9 class, I taught the same lesson as I had the previous one. About ten minutes into the lesson, I noticed a glazed expression on many faces and a certain amount of shuffling going on. One or two students had knowing smirks on their faces. One student finally put up his hand and told me what the problem was. This sounds like terrible incompetence on my part but it's a fairly common experience. When you're working with many classes, some of whom will be in the same year band following the same Scheme of Work, it's easy to become confused. No matter how secure you are in your mental organisation, you mustn't rely on this alone. One momentary slip and you could be in the same position I was.

Maintaining continuity for one class as a whole is very easy: your planning documents become your recording documents. As you teach a lesson, put a tick against or a line through the lessons in your week by week planner and, if you like, additionally, on your term by term planning sheet (Figure 2). If, as often happens, you begin another lesson early because you've progressed faster than you expected or you have to carry some lesson contents over because the class has not progressed as quickly as you hoped, then you need to use the review, memo and connection with previous work sections on your individual lesson planner sheets (Figure 3) to record this. If you find that after a few sessions, your week by week planning is becoming seriously out of step with the actual speed of your teaching, then you need to make appropriate adjustments. Otherwise you may lose your overall sense of the students' progression, and also you may need to alter the date of resource bookings.

Never impede or rush a class, merely to bring them into line with your planning. Obviously, other circumstances might make this necessary, but the fact that your planning is not synchronous with the students' progression may be due to your misreading of their capabilities. In extreme cases of this, for example, your week by week planning being two or three weeks off schedule, you may need to go back and revise your planning from long term down to lesson by lesson.

Continuity on a student by student level

Continuity on a student by student level is slightly more demanding, tied up, as it is, with attendance monitoring and assessment. In our school, it is policy that all subject tutors keep a register of attendance for every lesson they teach. This policy is fairly common but not universal. We suggest that if your school hasn't adopted it, you should. You need to have available, without recourse to centrally stored form registers, your own record of attendance, so that you can identify students who've missed lessons and compensate them for this, either with extra work, consultation or instructions via another student. If you have a student who is underachieving, evidence of poor attendance is good ammunition to have, should your teaching be called into question.

Progression within classes

On a whole-class level, progression is really taken care of at the planning level. As we have said in the planning section above, by making schemes of work educationally coherent, as well as making them hit assessment objectives, you will ensure progression at the class level. However, just because a class has received a lesson does not mean that it has progressed automatically. You need to sample their progression on a regular basis. This is best done on a student by student basis.

Formal assessment is part of the teaching process, but it may not happen often enough for you to have a full picture of each student's progress. Also, strictly speaking, formal assessment that may be part of a final national examination grading, should not be used for diagnostic purposes; the diagnosis needs to have been done leading up to the formal assessment. In addition to assessing students, you should be monitoring their progress and diagnosing any problems they have and suggesting solutions. You should be diagnosing and acting on your diagnosis long before you get to the formal assessment stage.

There are many ways to go about this. If you use a lesson planning document similar to the one shown above (Figure 3), you will have determined and recorded your aims and objectives for the lesson. It is important that these aims and objectives are clear and meaningful. It is sometimes tempting to put something along the lines of, 'To get through an hour and ten minutes relatively calmly', or, 'To fill up the last lesson because we have finished the Scheme of Work'. Yet even a spare lesson at the end of a term should have something assessable, formally or informally, in it, even if it's only a game that reinforces interpersonal communication or encourages student interaction. If you have clearly stated aims and objectives, then you will have clear indicators of progression. To pick up these indicators, there are several options open to you.

1 Marking – although you shouldn't always include a written component in every lesson (this obviously will depend on your subject area), the regular setting and marking of written work will give a detailed knowledge of the progress of each student. Remember though, marking is meant also to guide students, so always make sure your written comments are meaningful to them. Your comments should be related to your aims and objectives, and this should be communicated to your students.

2 Student consultations – we firmly believe this is the most under-used method of informally assessing the progress of students. In some subjects, for example, English and modern languages, this method can also be used for formal assessment. Talking to your students, and discussing both your view and theirs, regarding their progress, is illuminating, sometimes startling, and a major contributor to good relationships with classes. For us, it is the single most productive method of interaction with students. Obviously, with pre-Year 12 class sizes in many secondary schools running at about thirty, this is a time-consuming activity, but time must be made for it. I normally conduct my individual consultations when the rest of the students are working on their next piece of written work, shortly after I have returned their books after marking the previous piece.

This has three advantages:

- it gives feedback that can be applied to their current work in progress
- it ensures that they have understood the comments and advice marked on their work
- it provides an opportunity verbally to affirm students (*always* find something to affirm) in addition to the written commendations they receive.

We suggest that you conduct these consultations on an individual basis, calling students up to the teacher's desk one by one, while the rest of the class are doing written work. If you attempt to consult with students individually while other students are engaged in paired or group discussion, you'll find you have to spend too much time monitoring the rest of the class, thereby short-changing the individual students of the attention they need and deserve.

3 Question and Answer sessions – these are useful to enliven the lesson, particularly if there's been a lot of whole-class content teaching or a fair amount of writing. These sessions have the advantage of giving immediate information to the teacher as to how successful their lesson has been, without occupying too much time. They have the disadvantages of not necessarily sampling all the students' progression, and that they generally lead to no lasting record of progress. What we mean by this is, that the ebb and flow of a lively question and answer session is difficult to record fully; attempts to do so, either by mechanical means or on paper, can destroy spontaneity. The disadvantage of not always sampling all student's progression is unavoidable. No matter how warm and encouraging a teacher is, there are some students who will not speak in front of the whole group and for whom even the prospect of doing so is a cause of great anxiety. Although this is a problem that needs to be addressed at some point, it must be done with great care. Too much pressure applied to an orally reluctant student can cause her or him to dread and despise your lesson, and ultimately become educationally deaf to it. With students like this, individual consultations provide a more effective means of relating to them.

Sometimes you may also get a whole class who do not respond to your questions. You must then examine the type of questions you are asking. One of the pieces of advice often given to new teachers, is to ask open questions rather than closed ones. Open questions have no fixed answer, and allow the student to respond in their own way; whereas closed questions have only one or a narrow range of answers. Open questions are sometimes useful because they encourage greater reflection in the student. Conversely, closed questions often elicit the parroting back of given information. This advice needs to be accepted with some reservation. It's good advice if you and the class have confidence in each other. If, however, the students are unfamiliar with each other, which is a common occurrence in setted classes (by this we mean, classes that have been formed on the basis of an assumed shared level of ability in a particular subject or subjects), unfamiliar with you, as they will be at some point, or, most important, are unsure of what you have just taught them, they might find open questions threatening.

If confronted by an unresponsive class, begin with closed questions, even down to the level of yes/no questions, praising warmly any answers, until the students' level of confidence is raised. Never get angry with an unresponsive class and never panic yourself into answering your own questions before they've had a chance to respond. In that context, a reasonable wait time, say, five to ten seconds, between stating the question and asking for a response, can be very effective. A class needs to be worked sensitively.

If, after all your efforts, the class still won't respond (this is very rare), you might try to engage individual students in consultation to find out what's going on. You may find the whole class is worried about the Maths examination that follows your lesson, that the whole class has been punished unfairly by another teacher and the students have withdrawn their labour, that another student they know has been killed or injured, or that you've 'pitched' the lesson wrongly and they haven't understood a word of what you've said.

4 Tests – these are an obvious and common method of checking individual student progress, but they have to be used carefully. They can easily seem threatening to some students and make them conservative in their learning style. We mean by this, that they may concentrate too much on securing what they've already earned, rather than being hungry for more. I often disguise tests as pub style quizzes to give them a flavour of friendly competition. If you're teaching mixed-ability classes (in reality, all classes are mixed ability) beware of over-publicising test results because this can reinforce the poor self-image and low self-esteem that the least able in the class may have, and, conversely, inflate the sometimes over-confident egos of the most able.

If the test, rather than a formal assessment, is just for the purpose of checking how the work is going, try and design it so that it can be marked by the students themselves. You don't need more marking, and the results of tests are more quantitative than qualitative; hence the feedback given to the students rarely amounts to more than highlighting areas of insufficient learning.

Continuity and progression between classes

If you are employing the above planning/recording methods, this continuity and progression is more or less achieved already. If you have your planning documents and your records for each individual class and student, all you have to do is compare one similar class's data with another. How this is done is really up to you, but the point we want to make is that adequate recording of continuity and progression for each class essentially supplies the data for continuity between classes. Of course, theoretically, similar classes can progress at different rates, but as long as this is recorded on your planning documents, continuity is assured.

Continuity and progression between subjects

The carrying out of the above planning/recording procedures, ensures that this occurs.

Continuity and progression: additional thoughts

As you can see, control of continuity and the maintenance of progression is a vital part of becoming an effective teacher. It is important though, whether you adopt our method of maintaining continuity and progression with your classes or one of your own, that it is not so time-consuming as to encroach on other vital activities, such as planning and marking. One of the criticisms of the National Curriculum is that, with its emphasis on extensive recording, it has done just this. Keep your systems simple, and build them into your planning and teaching. Make them work for you. If your continuity is perfect, then you will project confidence and professionalism to your students. If you know how each student is progressing, then they will know they are cared for and monitored. As a result, you will have a better relationship with and more commitment from them.

Pitching

In DfE criteria 2.3.3 and 2.3.4, it is stated that the competent teacher needs to set appropriately demanding expectations for students and employ a range of teaching strategies appropriate to the age, ability and attainment level of students, respectively.

These are more commonly referred to, in teaching, as 'pitching'. We have never known whether this is a musical or a cricketing analogy, but what it means is, to ensure that what you're teaching and the various styles you employ to do it, are suited to your particular classes. The next chapter deals with the choice of methods (for example, whole-class, group or individual teaching etc.) in a class-management context, and we don't want to cover the same ground here. The method you use to teach a particular component of your course is often determined by the content, but the amount of support you give to it, in terms of teacher introduction and guidance, depends entirely on how you 'pitch' the lesson.

For example, if I were teaching a poem to a Year 9 class, with the aim of getting them to explore both its surface and hidden meanings, I would have a choice of:

- going through it with them line by line and asking them to interpret it for me, and, if they came up with nothing, giving them my interpretation
- picking out a few significant parts for them and explaining the parts, then putting the class into pairs, and asking them to find other similarly significant parts, and to report back to me towards the end of the lesson
- dividing the class into groups of four, issuing the poem, instructing them to read it, and seeing what meaning they can obtain from it, giving no guidance at all.

These three different ways of teaching a poem, roughly coincide with the three different levels of 'pitching': low, middle and high. 'Pitching' low is often described as keeping the least able with you. This has the advantage of making sure the self-esteem of the least able students in the class is not damaged and that there is no anxiety about not understanding in your classroom. It has the disadvantage of denying the impetus of a challenge to average and high ability members of the class. 'Pitching' middle, which roughly coincides with the second method of teaching the poem, has the advantage of challenging the majority of the class. However, it may leave the least able alienated and the most able still under-stretched.

To compensate for this, the teacher would have to circulate around the classroom, aiding the strugglers and pushing the under-stretched to greater heights. This is a good method, but very exhausting and not always practical. The third method of teaching the poem, coincides with 'pitching' high. This method will either succeed dramatically and really stimulate the class with the most able feeling at home (remember the able student has special needs too), the students of average ability rising to the challenge, and the least able needing support, which they may get from other members of their groups (if you organise your groups with care) rather than you.

If you're teaching setted groups, where you don't have the extreme variations in ability that you get in a very mixed ability class, you'll still have to give some thought to pitching because all classes will have a range of abilities. If you're teaching to a truly mixed ability class (for example, at present I teach a Year 7 class in which there are four students who have a reading age of less than seven, and one student with a reading age of seventeen or above), you might consider these choices in your teaching:

- set differentiated tasks for the most and least able and pitch at the middle
- set tasks that are capable of being done at varying degrees of complexity, and pitch as you judge appropriate.

We make it sound as if selecting the correct 'pitch' is easy. The fact is that even extremely experienced teachers, occasionally pitch their lessons wrongly. This is less of a problem provided you recognise the symptoms of inappropriate pitching. If you've pitched too low, your class will probably begin to shuffle, glance at their watches and look annoyed. If you're pitching too high, you'll probably get dead silence and thirty pairs of eyes staring at you in terror. There could be other reasons for these reactions, but, provided you're a well organised, reasonably entertaining teacher, the most likely cause is that you've chosen to teach your lesson at an inappropriate level. If this happens, you need to adjust your approach on your feet. Never keep going regardless, particularly in the latter case, because you'll only have to go over that lesson again.

Whatever the attainment levels of the students, all of them will get much more out of lessons if you present your subject in clear language and in a stimulating manner.

Presenting your subject

DfE criterion 2.3.5 requires newly qualified teachers to present subject content in clear language and in a stimulating manner. One is tempted to comment when reading this, 'Well obviously! But how?' Like a lot of the criteria for teaching competencies, this vague statement might be welcomed for its lack of prescription. However, its very permissiveness can lead to a commensurate lack of confidence in the new teacher, precisely because of its vagueness. We will deal with the two halves of this statement separately, to clarify things more clearly.

Clear language

One of my most treasured memories of being involved with student teachers, happened when I was observing an English lesson given by one of them. An excellent student teacher, she was presenting some information to a rather excited Year 7 class. Although most of the students were attentive, one or two were carrying on spirited conversations of their own. The student teacher talked over them (something to be avoided at all costs) for a while, then snapped something along the lines of, 'I do wish certain miscreants would refrain from interjecting whilst I am in the process of informing you of your set task.' She was greeted with the silence she wanted, but through boggle-eyed bewilderment rather than understanding. One hand went up, 'What exactly are we supposed to do Miss?'

Although amusing, the above example illustrates a trap most of us fall into at some time or other in our teaching. Formal and complex language might be a simple way of raising the register of our utterances, making them sound authoritative and imposing. Adopting formal registers of speech is a way of enhancing our authority in the classroom but it's a two-edged sword; it can alienate and confuse our students. Merely by training to be teachers, more often than not after following a degree course, we've all had a greater than average exposure to elevated and formal registers of language and probably associate these with 'proper' education. Some of us will carry this into the classroom. It would be very interesting to know though, what percentage of teachers' language is understood by their target audience.

In practical terms, this is a very important area. Obviously, you shouldn't use the same level of language for a Year 13 class of A Level Psychology students that you do for a Year 7 mathematics class, but you shouldn't talk down to either class. Clarity is not a function, necessarily, of brevity. Some four word sentences (for example, 'Please eradicate obvious errors') are much more complex than longer sentences (for example, 'Please read what you've written to see if you've made any mistakes'). Restricting your vocabulary and your sentence variety, may make your presentation dull, and, in addition, stop you from achieving competency in criterion 2.3.6, developing students' language and communications skills.

So, what are we to do? Once again, this is a situation where you need to be flexible. Never regard even the most formal of teacher-led lessons, as a one way process. Even when lecturing, make sure you are monitoring the students, in terms of observing them, their body language and facial expressions (yawning, scratching and nudging the person next door are not good signs; be careful here though: animated doodling may be a sign of engagement, as may be a puzzled frown), and asking them regular questions about what you're saying. Don't rely on them to tell you they don't understand; a lot of students are very sensitive to your feelings, and wouldn't want to tell you that you've gone way over their head. Don't stick to scripts, and be prepared to rephrase what you've said as many times as necessary, to get the message across.

A note of warning here. Sometimes what you are saying is unclear because you might not have what you want to say clear in your own mind. There is no substitute for thorough preparation. Never try to muddle your way through complex issues. If it's not clear to you, it won't be clear to the students, no matter how you phrase it.

One particular method I use to avoid problems with the clarity of my language, is to say something once in a high register (for example, Freud said, 'That underlying every mental event there must be a corresponding molecular event'), and then to automatically restate the same thing, in a lower register (for example, that is, for everything you think or feel, bits of your brain must be doing something). This has two advantages.

1 It can be used to comic effect. On particularly dry and dusty material, I play up the contrast between the formal and informal, maybe adopting a different persona for each register (for example, 'To be or not to be ...' becomes, 'To top myself or not ...').
2 It contributes to the development of the students' language and communication skills, by not depriving them of access to more formal register and vocabulary, but without being confusing or bewildering.

We think an honest self-appraisal here is vital. Most of us are not used to analysing our own behaviour and vocal delivery to any great extent. It's essential, if you intend to teach, that you try to analyse yourself as carefully as possible. As with all things, have a realistic view of what can be achieved. To try to alter your public persona completely could be disastrous and lead to a collapse of confidence. But, on a basic level, if you have a quiet voice, you must reinforce silence while you are teaching, to make sure you are audible to all students. If you have a boring voice, and, let's face it, some of us do, you may need to inject more humour into your teaching. Use gesture and facial expression and modulate your voice, but don't go overboard, or you may discover the only thing your students have learned is how to do a passable imitation of you!

Try to avoid catch-phrases and unusual physical mannerisms. This is difficult, and you may need to be observed by a colleague in order to spot these. I was told on teaching placement by my university supervisor, that I sounded, when shushing the class, like a geyser, softly emitting little bursts of steam every so often. He suggested a variety of other techniques. I was quite affronted at the time, but later was very grateful. If a colleague does point out some personal quirk, don't be upset, be thankful. If your mannerisms include, continually folding and re-folding a piece of paper while you speak or finishing every sentence with the words '... and so on', you need to be told. Otherwise every Year 11 student you teach will be waiting for these quirks every lesson – and practising them afterwards in the corridor!

You may also need to be observed by a colleague to determine whether your voice is at the right volume. There is a myth that all teachers with quiet voices have discipline problems. Yet, provided you make a point of never talking over noise and insist on full attention when you're speaking, a fairly quiet but clear and audible voice needn't be a problem. In fact, a well-modulated, soft delivery can promote a classroom atmosphere of calm, attentive understanding and concentration. However, if you have a genuinely very quiet voice, do try to raise the volume. Otherwise, you will have to find a strategy for cutting through the noise that inevitably arises during some activities. Clapping your hands together or slapping the back of a board-rubber on a desk come to mind. Don't bang on the desk with your hand though: apart from frightening students (reason enough not to do it), one of the writers of this book thinks that this tactic damaged a tendon in his hand! Nor do we recommend a whistle in confined spaces, for obvious reasons. Beware too, of over-stretching your voice; it can make you more vulnerable to the throat infections which abound in the school population.

If you have a naturally loud voice, this is often perceived as an advantage in teaching. It can be, but it can also be your worst enemy. At some time, we think all of us have had a teacher or lecturer with an overly loud or shrill voice. It's a very unpleasant experience and we always have to suppress the urge to throw something or yell, 'Ah, shuddup!' Some people find loud voices make them fall asleep. Whatever the effect, an over-loud voice is not a sign of enthusiasm or control, but a problem. Very often, a bellowing delivery comes about because teachers have allowed noise to build up too much before correcting the situation or have allowed themselves to talk over students. In addition to the unpleasant effects this kind of voice has on its audience, it may also emphasise the distance between the teacher and student, and prevent any meaningful social exchange. It also means that, if a situation arises where a raised voice is needed for control purposes, you haven't really got anywhere left to go. Once again, get a colleague to observe you in action, and listen to their assessment openly.

If you've got an identifiable regional accent (don't forget a Hampstead or Home Counties accent is still a regional accent), it's nothing to worry about. A lot of rubbish is spoken by linguistically ill-informed people, some of whom work for the Government, about speaking 'properly'. These opinions are based on value-judgements, not knowledge about the clarity of different regional accents. Provided your students can clearly hear you and understand you, your accent should be celebrated. Standard English, the chosen dialect of the self-styled 'educated classes', can be spoken in any accent.

Stimulating presentations

We have been spellbound by a teacher using just a voice and a chalk-board, and stultified by a multi-media, laser pointer, interactive video presentation. Being able to give a well-paced and well-presented lecture, is an important competency for all teachers to acquire because there may be occasions when all you have available is just yourself and your students. Use all the techniques you can: humour, rhetorical questions, actual questions, ludicrous examples and so on. If, however, other devices and resources are available, by all means use them, but ensure that they're suitable or appropriate for the lesson you're giving. More importantly still, ensure that you're familiar with their use. Nothing is more frustrating for a student than being halfway through reading an overhead projector slide and the teacher whipping it off the machine and putting on another one. Nothing provides as good an opportunity for disruptive hilarity and time-wasting, as a teacher spending half the lesson trying to coax a video recorder into life. If you're unfamiliar with your chosen resources or believe that you're one of those people who doesn't get on with mechanical things, either take the time to learn how to use the equipment beforehand or don't use it at all.

Remember, ultimately, you and your rapport with the class are the most important resources you have and any other visual or teaching aids you use should contribute to, not replace, these. Never plan a 'bells and whistles lesson' just for novelty value.

Clear language and a stimulating style are worthy assets in their own right. These qualities also help effective teachers to get the best out of their students in terms of language growth and communicative efficiency.

Developing language and communication skills

DfE criterion 2.3.6 highlights the importance of being able to contribute to the development of students' language and communication skills. Obviously, some of what we have said in the previous section is relevant to this. Just by being clear and well organised in your presentations, both written and spoken, you'll enhance the language and communication skills of your students. But this contribution by 'osmosis', so to speak, is not enough to fulfil criterion 2.3.6 by itself. We'll discuss the issue in two separate sections: written communication and spoken communication.

Written communication

The school we work in, very sensibly, has a whole-school correction policy for written English. This gives students a uniform standard by which to measure their writing and ensures that they attend to their writing skills in all subjects. Some teachers, sadly, and some schools, even more sadly, still believe that the correction and development of written English is the sole preserve of the English teacher. If this were ever true, from criterion 2.3.6, it clearly no longer is. Don't despair, though, if, as a physics or mathematics teacher, you have visions of having to assess a poem on starlit nights or an essay entitled 'What I did on my summer holidays'. This is not the case. Clearly, this competence is restricted to the kind of written communication appropriate to your subject area, for example, the right organisation, appropriate clarity and correct spelling of technical terms in an experimental report.

Depending on your school's policy, you may correct and advise on general issues of punctuation, grammar and spelling. However, in terms of assessment, be careful that you don't include these features of a student's work in an assessment, unless the syllabus or Statements of Attainment you are working from specify so. This is particularly important when you're working with less able students, who may be very talented in areas other than English. To penalise these students wrongly, for a poorly punctuated or spelt piece of work, may deny them one of their rare opportunities to shine. Similarly, to let gross written errors pass, because a piece of work still fulfils your assessment criteria, may be reinforcing errors that will cause your students to be discriminated against later.

One way of reinforcing good written practice, is to make sure any written communication made by you, is correctly spelt, punctuated and, as far as possible, in Standard English. Not all of us are at home on paper, and some of us are very tense about it indeed. However, apart from it being professional to produce immaculate written English, it can also be important in terms of class control. I well remember the contempt that one teacher from my own school days was held in, because of the poorly spelt and randomly-capitalised messages he sent. If you're worried about this, get yourself a pocket dictionary and maybe ask a colleague to look over anything you write for general consumption. There's nothing shameful in this latter strategy: I do it as a matter of course because often the person who actually writes something is the least likely person to spot any resulting errors.

Spoken communication

We have dealt with the teacher's side of this in a preceding section: *Clear Language*. It remains for us to deal with the teacher's role in the development of students' own communication. We must urge caution here. Peter Trudgill (1975) makes it clear that people whose accent or style of delivery is either heavily criticised or made to feel unwelcome, are likely to become unwilling oral contributors and, in extreme cases, could become electively mute in an educational environment. Never criticise accents or dialects in a public way and certainly never ridicule a student about these. Various government bodies have made noises, and there are certainly hints in the English National Curriculum document, that teachers should encourage the use of spoken Standard English.

Our view is that every student should be allowed a voice, and it should be their own. We admit that the ability to use Standard English in speech can be perceived as an advantage in our society. This is largely due to the fact that Standard English is perceived as the cultural capital of the middle and upper classes, and, in that respect, is seen to confer access to high status positions in society. Bearing in mind that this style of English can provide a passport to a better future, we think it's important that all students should be encouraged to learn it. An effective way to accomplish this, is through the use of role play ('You, Louise, are a BBC news reader, for this presentation.') or similar techniques, rather than by direct intervention.

Accent should not be tackled by you at all. People acquire the accent that is most socially useful to them as part of the socialisation process. No amount of classroom correction can work against important social influences in the long term, and it may do a great deal of damage to the self-esteem of the student. By all means, however, encourage clarity in your students' oral contributions. In the same respectful way you allow them to ask you to clarify your verbal material, so you should give them the opportunity to get their point across. Never move on from one student to another just because you don't follow what they've said; give them a chance to re-phrase it. This is essential for your relationship with the students, but, don't forget, the students need to be considerate with each other too.

When your students are in discussion amongst themselves, monitor turn taking and make sure that particular students do not dominate the others. Everyone should know that they can contribute. The human resource of social interaction, is the single most important aspect of the teaching process, but sometimes this process can be enhanced by the additional use of other resources. These must be chosen and deployed with care.

Selecting and using appropriate resources

In DfE criterion 2.3.7, it is stated that the competent teacher needs to: demonstrate ability to select and use appropriate resources, including Information Technology.

We've said quite a bit already about the use of resources and the necessity of using them with care in terms of supporting a lesson. In that respect, we've been speaking mainly about resources used by you to enhance your presentations. There are, of course, other resources (for example, photocopied handouts, special scientific equipment, textbooks, A4 paper etc.) that are used by students in the tasks you give them. You must have a firm control of these resources and a good idea of why you want to use them. If, for instance, you issue a photo-copied handout, you must tell the students whether they are to write on those or in their exercise books. If you issue a set of textbooks, make sure you know how many you've issued, and count them back in again at the end of the lesson. From a purely control point of view, this managing of procedures, will affirm your position in the class-room as the person in overall charge.

Some subjects are more resource intensive than others. PE, science, CDT, art and performing arts teachers are well aware of the plethora of resources they have to issue and orchestrate every lesson. For them, it must occupy a significantly greater amount of planning time and time in the lessons for setting-up and clearing-up. For these particular subjects, there are special Health and Safety elements too. You must be familiar with all the rules and regulations, and adhere strictly to them in every classroom. Failure to do so, could result in injury or, in extreme cases, death of a student. Never forget, that – apart from the obvious tragedy that might result from negligence on a teacher's part – if you're in breach of Health and Safety regulations, it may be you, as well as the school, who is liable.

In the interests of conserving your energy, and ensuring that class-room time is predominantly used for learning, be parsimonious with resources. Don't use five where one will do; otherwise, you'll spend all your time counting things in and out. Do use your students (choose them with care, though!) to help you with the distribution of these devices, provided their assistance in the setting up of props etc. doesn't constitute a Health and Safety risk. This gets the students involved in the management of learning, but make sure that you also do some of the menial work, to show that it has to be done and that no one is above doing it: an important lesson in life.

We reiterate that resources should not be used for their own sake. A lesson, if it's dull, won't be lifted by lots of resources; it will just be a dull lesson that has lots of extra work attached to it. Only use resources, like tools, for specific jobs. Properly used, additional resources will improve the standard of your teaching and may increase your productivity. IT resources particularly contribute to this.

IT for professional development

Although many schools are still severely under-resourced in terms of Information Technology, increasingly IT usage is becoming a part of the teacher's life, both in terms of teaching and personal productivity. We know some of you will throw up your hands in horror and say things like, 'But I don't understand computers!' or 'Computers don't like me!' We sympathise with these sentiments. Often people are not properly introduced to IT, either due to poor training or no training at all. Often computers are locked away in rooms or cupboards or used constantly by another department. There may be lists of 'authorised' users and rules about who may or may not use the equipment. These days are numbered. IT is given weight in the National Curriculum, both as a subject in its own right and across the curriculum. The emphasis is on using IT as a productivity tool, rather than as a body of knowledge in itself.

It is essential that you, the intending teacher, bite the IT bullet (many of you already have, we know). Grab any opportunity given to you for IT training. If you can, borrow a computer from your school over the holidays and get to know it. Try to get some tutoring time with colleagues or students who are proficient with IT, to introduce you to the basics. Pick these tutors with care though. IT is often still in the hands of people who see it as a way of enhancing their status and are reluctant to give all and sundry their 'special' knowledge. Sadly, these 'what's mine is mine' individuals, are, all too frequently, teachers. Students are usually more gracious and more patient, when it comes to sharing their IT knowledge base with beginners. However, the increasingly intuitive design of IT, and its high status in the National Curriculum, are factors that are making the hoarder types, dinosaurs on the verge of extinction.

Incidentally, don't feel threatened if there are students present in a class who know more about computers than you do. Use these students to help you; they'll enjoy this, and it will help you cope with the lesson. This kind of relationship makes some teachers uneasy because they feel that their authority rests on knowing more than their students at all times. We believe they are mistaken. Your authority rests in who you are and your rapport with your students. We have often used knowledgeable students to help us with IT, and they've never seen it as an opportunity to assert themselves in unproductive ways. Furthermore, recalcitrant students often relate to computers in a very positive way, using them as 'equal status peers' rather than as 'hectoring' teachers.

A whole book could be written about the uses of IT in education alone, and many issues are out of our scope here. But we'd like to mention a few more things. Whenever IT is mentioned in the educational sphere, it's always spoken about as a resource for teaching. This is only half the story. One area that is almost never mentioned is the use of IT for your own personal productivity. Personally, I use a word-processor to produce all my memos, letters and reports, improving the professionalism of my presentation and the ease of repetitive production. I use a spreadsheet to present, sort and analyse class lists against assessment levels. I use a desktop publisher to design worksheets and departmental notices. I use a data-base to keep track of my classroom library. By doing this, it helps me to maintain a standard of presentation and improves my efficiency because, once these systems are in place, they can be applied year after year. After an initial injection of effort, these easy to learn routines, will simplify and ease your teaching life. Additionally, it is clear that the use of IT, as a means of becoming more personally productive, is the way things are going in general. Some education authorities are already installing electronic registers and computer processed reporting systems. Moreover, the National Curriculum increasingly insists on the use of IT for students in real-life situations. The more IT can be built into your work and that of your students, the better it will be for you and for them.

What your mentor should do for you

OBSERVATION

Watching good teachers teaching their subject is a joy. We only wish we had more chances to do this now that we are qualified. But teachers are not usually too keen to have their peers watching them when they practise their craft. So make sure your mentor arranges plenty of opportunities to see effective teachers in action. As a student, you will be granted that privilege because you will be regarded as an apprentice rather than a judge. Your observation schedule should include opportunities to do the following:

- see some of the teachers' lesson plans. This can be a sensitive area because some of them have dispensed with those 'neater than neat' plans which students are expected to produce for visiting university tutors on demand. That said, effective teachers do have their plans and their strategies, so ask to see, as diplomatically as possible (a good mentor should be able to help here), whatever they use, and, with their permission, take photocopies of what you think might work for you. We like to produce dual purpose lesson plans which double as a schema for us and as a resource (that is, a handout) for our students
- get some longitudinal observation in; that is, watch a teacher taking the same class over a period of time. This will help you to get a more secure handle on those teaching strategies which effective teachers use to maintain continuity and progression in the courses they teach
- ensure that you observe teachers working across wide ability and age ranges. This is vital if you want to develop your pitching skills. At the very least, you should have watched lessons given to students in Years 7, 9, 11,12 and 13
- shadow teachers who use a lot of IT in their teaching. When you want to learn a particular skill, for example, creating a file on earthquakes, ask the teacher to take you through each step of the process, using the keyboard and mouse yourself, and write down each sequence in a notebook. This is an instance when observation and practice merge. Here's an example of what might follow in terms of what you do and what you write in your notebook: Click on Microsoft Works; Click on File; Click on Create New File; Click on Word Processor; Key in your data on Earthquakes; Click on File; Click on Save As; Key in EQuakes (seven digits maximum, and no spaces); Click on OK: you're done! What's more, you can retrace your steps next time you need to create a different file.

PRACTICE
Ask your mentor if you can try your hand with these activities:

- preparing lesson plans that don't just look good but work well. 'Dry runs' can be tested on the mentor and other teachers, and, let's

face it, on the students. If possible, word process your lesson plans (capital letters make reading easier), and make a note of how well they worked (or otherwise!), and how long each activity took
- taking responsibility for teaching at least one class a particular aspect of their course over a clearly defined time span. This will give you the practical equivalent of your longitudinal observation. It will also help you to judge and measure the learning progress of your students, especially if you set and mark all their work for the part of the course that you teach
- matching your observation of teachers working with students of different ages and across different ability ranges with hands-on experience. The richer your teaching repertoire, the more skilful and confident you'll become, particularly, at getting the right pitch.

Action points

1 Make sure that your planning is sufficiently flexible, so you can cope with unfamiliar expectations.
2 Make sure you are familiar with existing schemes of work at your school, so you don't 're-invent the wheel'.
3 Ensure that you have matched your long-term planning against the expected assessment outcomes stipulated by your school, the examination board or the Government.
4 Make sure that your planning documents can also serve you as recording documents, to save you time in your busy schedule.
5 Divide your lessons up into different activities, to keep your students engaged.
6 Always explain your aims and objectives to your classes; that way, even seemingly dull or pointless tasks can be seen as productive.
7 Make sure that you are sufficiently flexible in your questioning approach to be able to draw a class into a discussion. Be prepared to ask 'closed' questions when necessary.
8 Be ready to alter the 'pitch' of your lesson if your class doesn't respond.
9 Get a colleague to listen to your vocal delivery and act on any advice they may have. Don't shout!
10 Avoid catch-phrases and 'ticks'.
11 Never criticise a student's accent or dialect.
12 Get your hands on IT as soon as possible.

CHAPTER 4

Class management

'Ms Khan, Can you go over this question again with me after school?'
'Miss, Joanne and Mark keep telling everyone I've got a free school dinner pass.'
'Sir, wouldn't it be better if we had the chairs in a circle instead of in rows?'
'Mrs Jordan, Joanna just swore at me.'

Students will often turn to you as an after-hours tutor, a personal counsellor, a dispenser of justice, a facilitator of learning and as an arbitrator of conflicts.

The DfE requires teachers to manage the learning and the behaviour of school students. It has stated this requirement as follows:

2.4 Newly qualified teachers should be able to:

2.4.1 decide, when teaching the whole class, groups, pairs, or individuals is appropriate for particular learning purposes

2.4.2 create and maintain a purposeful and orderly environment for the pupils

2.4.3 devise and use appropriate rewards and sanctions to maintain an effective learning environment

2.4.4 maintain pupils' interest and motivation.

Putting this into more concise terms, class management, as defined by the DfE, refers to: the ability to create a learning environment supported – as appropriate – by whole-class or other teaching arrangements, as well as by incentives and imposed rules, in which the interest and motivation of students are successfully engaged, and in which effective learning is given scope to flourish.

Ted Wragg (1993) rightly notes that teachers require competence in class management in order fully to display their other skills. For example, teachers need to decide when students should be taught as a whole class or when it's more important to encourage independent research alone or in groups, when certain types of student behaviour should be challenged and corrected openly or when a discrete, taken to one side, word in the ear is more appropriate. There are no right or wrong answers here. Teachers must use their class-management skills to make professional judgements that are most likely to produce maximum educational and behavioural benefits for the students.

The higher education institute and the schools where you'll spend time learning your craft, will expect you to acquire and develop class-management skills during your initial training. Nobody anticipates a 'finished product' when you first enter the classroom as a newly qualified teacher. However, an ability, at least, to handle the basics will already have been checked and 'certified'.

Being an effective class manager is akin to being a good coach: you will only get back from your students or players the responses that you have 'allowed' to flourish. It's your role, as class manager, to set the parameters, to get things rolling, to create an orderly environment (not necessarily, a quiet one) in which effective learning and good behaviour are encouraged to issue, to make it possible for great things to happen.

The DfE's first criterion on the class-management front is to calibrate the right teacher/student ratios for the different learning activities that occur in your classroom, gym, laboratory or wherever you practise your craft.

Whole class, groups and one-to-one

Put simply, you'll need to decide which organisational strategy – whole-class, group or individual teaching – is appropriate to the task at hand. These days, most teachers use all three methods.

Face this way

'Sit down, get out your pens and books, and face this way', was the usual routine in days gone by. Did anyone ever tell you how much time you had to spend in school listening to adults talk? Teachers still talk too much. In an average double lesson of seventy minutes, it's not uncommon for teachers to talk for at least an hour. This gives the students in the class – perhaps 30 of them – just ten minutes, shared between them, to join in the discussion. It's my policy to invite all the students I teach, to tell me what I'm doing right and what I'm doing wrong. Recently, some of them, very justifiably, told me to stop talking so much and to give them the opportunity to join in. There is a simple lesson here, which I've now acted upon: cut down on teacher talk by making whole-class teaching concise, brisk and to the point. This technique is especially well-suited to the introduction of new topics.

Here is how I put that philosophy into practice in my own lessons. I explain to my students that each topic will be introduced by a short lecture, and I issue them with my lecture notes (purposely written in a simple, easy-to-read style) before any teaching starts. I give them a few days' advance notice of each lecture and I ask them to read my lecture notes and suggested supporting literature beforehand.

I try to make the lecture a fun event by: bringing in suitable props, for example, fairly traded chocolate and coffee for the students to sample when teaching about trade between poor and rich countries; employing suitably engaging visual cues, like video clips from movies when lecturing on media representations of native Americans; and by adopting appropriate theatrical styles, for instance, wearing disguises (such jokiness doesn't always go down well though during the first stages of getting to know a class) when discussing the hazards of undercover research in social sciences. I also place considerable importance on making these whole-class sessions easy to understand, by linking theoretical issues to actual or simulated real-life events. The complex and sometimes remote language used to describe the uses and limitations of survey research, for example, can be made easier and more vivid by coming in with a clip board and an interview schedule and getting into some role play with the students:

'Now tell me, Karen, how often do you sing in the bath – Always/Occasionally/Never?'

The introductory lecture lasts for about twenty minutes (audience concentration tends to wane after that), and it's followed by an open discussion (which lasts for as long as the students want). After the lecture and the discussion are over (which might take up several lessons), I ask the students once again to read my lecture notes and to consult other relevant sources, for example, key sections in their textbooks. Doing this reading, both before and after the lecture, helps the students to 'over-learn', thereby enhancing their knowledge and understanding.

Then we're ready for the next stage: a whole-class briefing which provides advice, directions and guidelines for the mainly independent activities that follow. At this stage in the proceedings, be prescriptive about some things, for example, the safe use of scientific equipment, and consultative about other things, for example, 'How do you suggest we conduct a school survey on vegetarianism?' Once group or individual work is up and running, it's useful to employ short bursts of whole-class teaching when students raise questions or encounter difficulties which suggest that certain important issues require further elaboration. The knack here is to avoid sudden intrusions that upset the impetus of independent research. To avoid such distractions, you might have to save a five or ten minute slot at the end of each lesson for additional whole-class inputs. Once the teaching of a particular topic is nearing completion, it's helpful to revisit the ground that has already been covered with a short rounding off lecture. This tidies up any loose ends. It also provides a good opportunity for another whole-class question and answer session, as well as a final summary.

Provided it is used appropriately and concisely (generally, from between five to twenty minutes), whole-class teaching is a superb instructional style. Certain stages of a lesson cannot be properly managed in any other way. Suppose, for example, you're taking a Year 7 class French lesson. The introduction of new language very easily lends itself to some preliminary 'listen and repeat' drills, where the teacher provides a good language model and all the students learn through choral repetition (many of them find this very enjoyable). A great advantage of this teaching approach is that the students' attention is very focused and they all work to the same beat. On the negative side, if whole-class drilling exercises are over-used, student autonomy goes out of the window, and boredom sets in. That's why whole-class teaching should be viewed as an important instrument in a mixed toolbag, which also contains group and individual learning strategies. Before considering these other strategies, here are a few reminders on when to use whole-class teaching. Use it as:

- a scene setter that introduces a theme and provides guidance for independent research, before handing things over to group and individual work
- a short-burst adjunct to independent learning that is used when students raise problems that require whole-class explanations
- a curtain closer that goes over the main issues, invites further questions and provides clear answers
- a 'listen and repeat' drill device (particularly suitable in modern foreign languages) that locks all the class into the same pace and rhythm.

While whole-class teaching can be a very effective way of promoting learning, don't think of it as a purely one-way means of communication. Encourage your students to cut in and ask questions as your lecture proceeds. Pause now and then, and throw out questions to the class, and to individual students by name. It's also important to make your talks exhilarating by communicating your enthusiasm and excitement about the issues under consideration. Use your voice well, speaking audibly, clearly and vibrantly. Move around the classroom, offer a smile here and some eye contact there. Here's your chance. You've got an audience. Entertain them. Now on to group work.

Re-arranging the desks

We hope you don't think that group work in classrooms turns the teacher into a meandering facilitator, an incidental resources person whose job consists of pointing students in the right direction, and leaving it at that. Effective teachers keep close track of independent learning activities. They move unobtrusively from group to group, listening, registering, monitoring. These teachers accept that student talk and interactive activities are key elements in effective learning. They also use their class-management skills to suggest realistic schedules for tasks to be completed, and they offer that very precious resource, their subject knowledge, to students who want to tap it.

Group work can provide an excellent medium for unlocking the

89

inner thoughts of students, especially when the teacher invites them to bring their own ideas openly into the forum. It's immensely gratifying for teachers to see normally quiet students no longer content, in the heat of a group debate, to leave their beliefs and convictions outside the classroom door. Students have a right to feel passionately and to think profoundly. Don't stifle those qualities by putting down independent thought. The apathy which arises in students reared on a diet of 'teacher knows best', drilled instructions is a powerful disincentive to self-motivated learning. So encourage your students to be critical and to rebut your arguments when they think you've got it wrong. That way, you'll encourage much more open debate, thereby enhancing the confidence of the students to air their views in public.

Once you've decided to make group work a part of your teaching repertoire, you'll need to concentrate on group selection, group size and classroom layout. There are no fixed rules about how to decide which students should make up each of the groups and what size they should be. But here are a few pointers.

- Friendship groups based on student choice often work well because co-operativeness and cordiality are usually assured. There's always the risk though, similar to when students pick games teams, that a few unfortunates will be left standing on the sidelines. This can be very damaging to the self-esteem of the affected students.
- Mixed ability groups based on teacher selection is an excellent arrangement. This model is good for low, middle and high-level achievers because it encourages peer tutoring. When students teach other students, the student tutors come to understand more about the things they teach in the process of teaching the student tutees. Teaching others is always a great teacher itself. Moreover, the tutees make learning gains because their tutors can readily relate to them on a student to student level.
- Four is a good group size. It avoids the problem of a dyad and an outsider formation, which can occur in groups of three. Marginalisation of 'odd ones out' can also arise in groups with other odd numbers, and should be avoided if possible. Pairs work well because mutual dialogue is encouraged.

As far as the classroom is concerned, if you're fortunate, you'll do all or most of your teaching in one room. In that case, you can arrange the layout of the room to support the kind of activities you want to provide. Even if you have to teach in different rooms, you'll have some scope to shift the furniture. It doesn't take long to move a few desks together and to re-arrange some chairs. If you want to get students to help you with this, check what the school policy is on moving furniture first. You might find, for Health and Safety reasons, that this can only be carried out by members of staff.

Our preferred layout is putting most desks together to make a giant, boardroom-style, rectangular table with chairs set around it. This seating arrangement gives everybody a sense of ownership in classroom activities. There are no rigid lines of demarcation, no teacher's desk standing between students and teacher. We also like a few clusters of desks scattered around the 'boardroom' table. They function as out-posts for independent study by groups or individuals, who can later re-join the 'boardroom' table when they want to report back their findings to the rest of the class. In practical terms, you'll probably find that the 'boardroom' table will only seat up to about sixteen students, so it won't be suitable for large classes.

When groups of students are busy working, don't remain glued to your chair. Walk about, engage them in conversation, share ideas with them, and show them you're interested in what they're doing. These tactics create a sense of engagement with the whole class. Being on the move – at least for some of the time – also adds to the ability of a teacher to scan the classroom and to pick up on what's happening. Moreover, you'll be better placed to spot and quickly defuse any mis-behaviour that might otherwise be out of sight to the sedentary, desk-dwelling teacher. Some commentators refer to this 'eyes in the back of the head' monitoring ability as 'withitness'. It's a skill well worth culti-vating – less, in our opinion, for its, 'We can see what you're up to' uses, more for its purposeful, rapport-generating qualities. It also allows a teacher to spot and commend the less obtrusive, good work by individual students.

Withitness is a general-purpose class-management skill. Acquire this skill and display it when you are lecturing, doing group work and whenever students are engaged at a task – either individually or inter-actively. However, if students are doing silent work – for example, during examinations – exhibit withitness less obtrusively. Too much movement on your part can be distracting to the students in these cir-cumstances. They will still be aware that you know what is going on if you maintain some occasional eye contact and generally look alert and in touch with your surroundings.

While it has many advantages, one of the problems with group work is that incorrectness can occur. In short, without the security of the expert teacher at the front of the class, students can sometimes get things wrong, give each other inaccurate information and even confuse their peers. Don't, however, let this shortcoming provoke undue anxiety. For one thing, students often get things right, and as long as they know they can call on you or their more knowledgeable peers for help when things get tricky, the problem is largely solved. Moreover, accuracy is not the only aim of effective teaching: co-operative and communicative skills are also important, and group work scores very highly indeed against these criteria.

That said, if students think they're doing something right, and it's clear to you they've got it wrong, you can either:

- employ an on-the-spot, interventionist correction (always essential if students are putting themselves and others at risk, for instance, using cooking oil in a way likely to start a fire during a home economics lesson)
- let the students persevere with their mistake if it seems likely that they'll eventually arrive at the right solution. This is an example of the commonly (and, in our view, mistakenly) criticised 'discovery approach' to learning, which actually has much to commend it. After all, the trial and error method is a generally accepted way of generating new knowledge.

But trial and error methods don't always sit easily with 'chalk and talk' types. We believe, though, that 'chalk and talk' is even more effective when it is supplemented with group work. Whole-class instruction, when concise and punchy, is fine. But it's not enough. Students also need the opportunity to work in groups. That way, they become active abettors in their own learning.

The next item for consideration, one-to-one teaching, will add another skill to your pedagogical stock.

One-to-one

One-to-one teaching underpins the educational practice of our ancient universities. The tutorial, as it's known in that setting, is an intellectual encounter between student and tutor, where each party has the other's undivided attention. It is intense, focused and rigorous, without distractions and it is the academic parallel of the apprenticeship. The accumulated knowledge of the tutor is made available to the student, who, in turn, is invited to learn, hone and practise the conferred wisdom under the expert eye of the 'master'.

At school, however, time-tabling arrangements make it very difficult to have students come by for tea, buns and a chat about Plato in the teacher's study. If you want to see students on a one-to-one basis, you will probably have to arrange a recess or after school appointment. If you are teaching students aged sixteen and above, you might also decide to meet when both of you are off timetable. Teachers in secondary schools normally have about three hours or so a week designated non-contact time. Older students will also probably have a similar amount of free study time. Other opportunities to see students individually, might arise if you are involved in collaborative teaching with another colleague who can look after the rest of the class while you do your one-to-one work.

A cautionary note is needed though. When I first started teaching in a north London comprehensive school, I was advised by the head-teacher never to work with a female student on an individual basis without others present. If false allegations of sexual misconduct are made after a male teacher has been alone with a female student, the teacher is placed in a very awkward and distressing position. You will have to form your own judgement about whether it is wise for a female teacher to be alone with a male student. Indeed, some of you might think it sensible to avoid being alone with an individual student under any circumstances. It is perfectly acceptable and common – for all kinds of reason (including the constraints placed on teacher time) to do individual teaching in ordinary class time. For example, you can set some group or whole-class work, and, while the students are doing it, you can conduct one-to-one teaching with students who need individual instruction.

Assuming you find professionally appropriate opportunities for individual teaching, what happens next? It's always a good idea to start the tutorial with a friendly opening gambit and with a comment or question that connects with the student's interests. Try also to find scope to offer some praise or encouragement: 'How are you today Maninder? I hear you're doing some community service in a Sikh nursery. Your fluency in Punjabi will help you a lot.'

When you begin to introduce a learning component into this personal dialogue, follow these procedures.

- Find out what the student can do. Ask a few questions to elicit responses. Remember that all students can do something well. Here's another chance to bolster the self-esteem of your student (a vital part of effective teaching), by praising achievement.
- Discover, in part, from the preceding responses, as well as from further probing, if the student is having difficulties with any aspects of the course. Here's an opportunity for you to hone your diagnostic skills (more about those in Chapter 5) and figure out where the 'blocks', if any, are occurring.
- Plan a personalised way forward for the student. This might involve, for example: supplementary assignments to be marked by you at an agreed time with the student alongside; pointing the student in the right direction on the resources trail; suggesting that the student might find it helpful to do collaborative work with some other student(s) in the class – both as a receiver and as a giver of educational benefits.
- Get the student to start at where she or he feels confident. In mathematics, for example, if the student is working from a book, let her or him choose a suitable point of entry. For some students, this might be at basic arithmetic level; others might already be on calculus.
- Encourage the student to ask other students for advice and assistance if necessary. Never underestimate the mutual gains that can arise when you get students to seek help from peers who are skilled enough to provide it. Avoid though only using student tutors for a student who is struggling; everybody, 'high-flyers' included, can benefit from some peer tutoring. As well as promoting effective learning, peer tutoring also fosters a warm, friendly, co-operative class atmosphere.
- Tell any student who runs into difficulties and who can't – or chooses not to – seek peer support, to ask you for help. Always – repeat, always – make sure that students can request your assistance whenever they need it. Make it very clear to all students that it's no embarrassment for them to turn to you, that it's your joy to help them, and that you're never put out by queries or questions – quite the contrary! Terrible damage can be done to a student's learning confidence if you're not perceived to be eminently approachable in

this crucial context. Incidentally, if a student comes to you because other students are equally confused, do some group or whole-class teaching to put matters right.

- Check the student's progress by asking her or him to let you know when she or he can handle a particular task, and have the student successfully demonstrate this. Lift the student's spirits by warmly applauding accomplishments (good for learning and self-esteem), and move her or him on to a further stage of the venture.
- Don't make the next task either absurdly easy or ridiculously difficult. Strike the right balance between these two extremes, but include an element of achievable challenge. Even when a student is working through a book, it's important not to assume that the next section is automatically self-evident. If it is, fine; if it's too easy or too difficult, improvise and set an appropriate assignment. Let the student work at her or his own pace. Pressure to go fast is bad for confidence and bad for progress. Make it very clear to all your students that achievement is about personal success. They should measure their progress against their own prior attainment, not against the performance of their peers.

With appropriate modifications, the techniques described above can be usefully applied to most subjects. Whatever you're teaching, the basic ingredients are to:

- have students start where they can achieve success. Let them decide the level
- encourage them to work at their own pace
- let them seek assistance, as appropriate, from their peers
- make them feel that they can always turn to you for advice and help, and that, by doing this, they're neither embarrassing themselves or troubling you
- ask them to tell and show you when they're successfully able to accomplish a specific task
- applaud their achievement and move them on to the next task, when they've demonstrated their competence to you
- make sure that the moved-on-to-task contains an element of achievable challenge
- get students to measure their success against their own progress from prior starting points, not against the learning curves of their peers.

The measure of your success as an effective teacher will be based on the extent to which your students are able to:

- increase their learning by achieving at their own pace
- enhance their psychological well-being by becoming aware of their progress
- develop their social skills by working in harmony with their peers.

Getting the right mix of whole-class, group and individual learning activities will increase the likelihood of these favourable outcomes.

The DfE also expects you to maintain students' interest and motivation within a purposeful and orderly learning environment, which is supported by the appropriate use of rewards and sanctions. The most important of these goals is keeping students interested and motivated because, when they like what they're doing, they learn more and play up less. It's also vital that your class management displays a purposeful, that is, task-oriented, atmosphere.

Interest, motivation and purposiveness

In large part, motivation is contingent on interest. Teachers who can harness the curiosity of their students are able to elicit a willingness of the students to learn. Interest-satisfying instruction motivates students far more effectively than coercing them into doing tasks they find irrelevant and boring. When students are fired up to learn because the prospect of doing so is exciting, they exhibit a readiness to persevere even when they encounter difficulties.

Don't over rely on motivating students by the promise of future rewards – a good job, decent pay and such like. Some students respond to this type of enticement in an instrumental, 'I'll do enough to get the grade I need' manner, without ever developing a sense of joy in the subject they're studying. It's more important to give your lessons an immediacy and an urgency that students can relate to in their real worlds right now. 'I know a lot of you like "techno music", so let's begin our study of electronics with some tracks from a "techno" band' (choose a band you know they like), will go down much better in terms of prompting an interest than, 'Let's study electronics today because some of you might work in that field when you leave school'.

It's also essential, as the DfE reminds us, to make your lessons purposeful. This means that what you get students to do should be focused rather than 'wishy-washy'. Helpfully, recent research (Bert P. M. Creemers, 1992) suggests that it's possible to identify the components of good, purposeful practice. Here is what the research says:

- maximise student-engaged time, that is, keep your students at the task to hand
- keep instruction direct and simple
- pace subject tasks in a step-by-step sequence (the 'walk before run maxim'), proceeding in small steps at a brisk pace
- expect students to make steady learning progress, and strongly convey that expectation (excellent for student morale)
- ask questions often and ask testing questions, where appropriate, giving immediate, corrective feedback.

Successful behavioural and learning outcomes are likely to have optimal effect when the above practices are combined rather than treated as discrete items. It's also important to motivate students without threatening them with sanctions. Unless we persuade students that what we ask them to do connects with their interests and their priorities, learning becomes abstract, dull and remote. And when that happens, the likelihood of students engaging in disruptive behaviour increases.

This last assertion is supported by research by Bill Badger (1992) into disruptive behaviour at a Cumbrian comprehensive school. From interviews of school students involved in 'high-level' disruptive incidents, Bill Badger found that boredom with the subject and an impatience with too much theory instead of practical application, were given as reasons for their misbehaviour. Pertinent to this issue, the 1988–9 Committee of Enquiry into Discipline in Schools (hereafter referred to as the Elton Report, after its Chair, Lord Elton) commented: 'Our evidence suggests that an important factor in promoting good behaviour among pupils is a curriculum which they see as being relevant to their needs.'

So make your lessons enjoyable and interesting, and link them to what the students can relate to and understand. This doesn't mean that everything you teach must have some immediate relationship with what's going on right now in the world outside the classroom. But your lessons should at least raise issues that go beyond the abstract and the remote. When you have to deal with theoretical issues, start things with discussions involving real events. For example, talk about what happens when we swim, before tackling Newton's Third Law of Motion. And – above all – generate a classroom atmosphere in which learning becomes fun.

Competent teachers are not the only creators of effective learning environments. A 15-year-old student with a good book, a 10-year-old student and some challenging software, might provide equally – or even more – compelling settings. But society expects teachers to be the experts on these matters, and pays them to compete successfully with other 'distractions', like interactive video games and satellite TV. And that is what you are up against these days: how to make a lesson on the English Civil War or on the use of the genitive case in Spanish as interesting and motivating as what can be obtained through activities outside of conventional classroom environments.

We say 'conventional' deliberately, because you might consider making your classroom an environment which does something different. You might make it a place that uses exciting technologies, a location where gripping debates and enthralling discussions take hold, where stuffy decorum and too much 'chalk and talk' beat a brisk retreat.

In today's high-tech, multi-media world, subjects often become more appealing, interesting and motivating when teachers use resources that students find entertaining. Illustrative of this point is a recent comic-book biography (complete with strikingly coloured drawings and speech balloons) of the Hitler years, recently (1991–2) trialled in German schools. The German Government's Centre for Political Education has invested heavily in the trials, and the book is regarded as an important weapon in the battle against the racist thuggery rampant in Germany at the moment. Evaluation of the reception of the book by school students aged 15 to 17, shows that the students got more out of its comic style than from standard history books. Its powerful visual impact initiated emotional and intellectual responses from students, which led to serious discussions and vigorous debates. All of this helped to fix the information in their minds.

The Hitler comic book forms part of a media package provided free of charge to teachers by the Bonn-based Centre for Political Education. The package also includes a computer game called, *Der Diktator,* in which players score by successfully resisting various stages of dictatorship.

When students enjoy what they are doing, great things happen.

Resources that galvanise and sustain students' attention are essential class-management tools. Make the most of them. They're not gimmicks, but abettors of motivation, effective learning, and orderliness. It's now time to have a more detailed look at this last characteristic because the creation and maintenance of an 'orderly' class environment is vital; it's also a DfE designated Competence.

Orderly environments

We hope you'll accept that orderliness doesn't have to mean a classroom in which an eerie silence prevails. Students should be encouraged to communicate, and when you have thirty people in a classroom that's bound to raise the volume. Some teachers create problems for themselves – and for their students – by insisting on absurdly quiet classrooms. Don't make this mistake – unless, of course, special circumstances (for example, doing examinations) require silence.

It would be wrong to think, however, that we're advocating an 'anything goes' policy. When you step into a classroom or make your presence known on any other part of a school premises, the vast majority of students you will come across, expect you to be a creator and an upholder of the institutional code of conduct. In that context, first entries and first impressions are very important.

First entries

Those crucial few moments – when you encounter a new class for the first time – should start setting a purposeful, orderly agenda for what's to come. Cutting things down to basics, you've got two main options: a formal, 'I'm in charge' entry, or an informal, 'Let's talk' entry. Of course, there are in-between approaches, but the real issue, as far as students' perceptions are concerned, can be put quite simply: 'Is our new teacher strict or easy-going?' We think the best way to deal with this matter is to be yourself, but if that's strict, don't be too strict. We begin kind and we try to stay kind, and we rarely adopt the 'start off tough and ease off later' approach. In fact, we believe that the most effective way to get the best out of all our students, as far as learning and personal and social development are concerned, is to treat them with compassion, courtesy and dignity. When students know that you're on their side, they rarely give you trouble.

Don't mistake an easy-going manner, though, with timidity and lack of orderliness. Try to make a fairly big public presence on that first encounter – whether you opt for the friendly smile entry or the firm business-like approach. Walk around the classroom, use your eyes to engage individuals or groups, speak in an audible, confident voice. In short, be assertive. It's also a good idea to tell your students how they should address you.

You might recall what I said about this matter in Chapter 2. The other student teacher on my teaching practice in a tough comprehensive school in Bethnal Green, invited the students to call him 'Mike' instead of 'Sir'. In a school whose culture did not encourage such liberal overtures, this was a big mistake. For all his genuine geniality, Mike had seriously misread the school's expectations governing teacher-student relationships. The quickest way to forfeit credibility in the eyes of your students is to do what Mike unwittingly did: break a ground-rule right from the outset. Mike's students called 'proper' teachers, 'Miss' or 'Sir'. That's how things were done, and that's what they expected. By doing the unexpected on this occasion, Mike lost the respect of his students. They interpreted his friendliness as a sign of weakness, and they played havoc with him.

There are, of course, schools that encourage students and teachers to be on a first name basis. In such an institutional culture, it would be equally inappropriate to insist on being addressed formally. The important thing is to 'go with the flow'. If you don't, you could be asking for trouble from some students. You're also likely to encounter resentment from other teachers for not adopting the school norm. As far as addressing your students is concerned, we strongly advocate calling them by their first names. If they prefer a shortened version, for example, Liz or Chris, use that. Learn their names as quickly as you can, and address them by name when you talk to them. They'll greatly appreciate this because it shows you regard them as individuals, not just as one of the class.

Forms of address and other important matters (for example, fire exit instructions) aside, don't feel that you have to launch into a, 'This is how I like things done, lay it on the line' talk straightaway. It's a good idea to introduce some teacher expectations into the first meeting, but students won't take kindly to a lengthy list of 'Do this' and 'Don't do this' commands.

Some rules of orderly conduct can be made clear if and when the need arises. Others can be raised without invoking a bossy tirade. For example, in an introductory science lesson, you might start off by telling the students that the department takes great pride in giving all its students opportunities to take active roles in practical lessons. You could inform them that equipment grabbing, and pushing to the front of the line doesn't happen in the science department. Point out that everybody gains – girls, boys, students who like science, students who think they don't like science (but that'll change!) – when everyone has an equal chance to get some real, hands-on experience with practicals. Most students we know have an impeccable sense of fair play, and this way of talking to them is likely to appeal to their sense of even-handedness.

Instead of dwelling too much on the 'dos' and 'don'ts' during that first encounter with a new class, tell your students about the exciting things they're going to learn in your lessons. Go to town on this theme. Your message to the students has to be as follows: 'I want you to enjoy my lessons because when you like what you're doing, you'll learn, you'll work and you'll succeed'.

But what if some of them still play up? What do you do then? In cases of low-level disruption, a plain, matter of fact, 'Get on with your work please', will often do the trick. But if things turn nasty, keep your cool and ask the student – politely – to do the same. Later in this chapter, we'll look at some of the best ways to handle students who are engaging in disruptive behaviour. First though, you'll be pleased to know that most misbehaviour is of a fairly trivial kind.

Types of misbehaviour

Don't pay too much attention to claims – often made in the tabloid press – that today's young people are more disorderly and troublesome than ever before. No doubt, newspapers in the Victorian age were reporting similar 'moral panics' about young people then. Press articles tend to concentrate on attacks on teachers by students, even though evidence suggests that such violence is relatively rare (Elton Report, 1989).

A national survey of primary, middle and secondary school teachers in England and Wales, commissioned by the Elton Committee and carried out during the first week of October, 1988, by social scientists at Sheffield University, puts things into perspective. For example, commenting on the frequency with which secondary school teachers said they dealt with misbehaviour 'during the course of their classroom

101

teaching the previous week', the researchers noted the following facts.

> Four pupil behaviours would appear to have been common experiences for the vast majority of secondary teachers. In each case they were reported as occurring by 80 per cent or more of those in the sample. At some point during the week, then, most teachers said they had had to deal with instances of pupils 'talking out of turn', 'hindering other pupils', engaging in 'calculated idleness or work avoidance' and 'not being punctual'.

These are the everyday types of student misbehaviour: hardly the stuff of tabloid 'louts on the rampage!' In fact, 'Physical aggression towards you the teacher', was at the bottom of the national survey's frequency of occurrence list. It was mentioned as having happened at least once during the week by only 1.7 per cent of the teachers. Outside of lesson times, 1.1 per cent of teachers reported some form of 'physical aggression' to them while conducting their duties around the school – again a very small percentage.

Naturally, we're concerned about any reports of physical aggression on the part of students towards teachers. But let's get things in perspective: dealing with 'heavy duty thuggery' is unlikely to be a prominent part of your work. The misbehaviour you'll most often encounter is of the relatively minor – but sometimes irritatingly persistent – low-level type. Talking out of turn, as , for example, when a student starts chatting about going to the movies after school instead of the different ways to greet people in French, will figure high on the list of the low-level but cumulatively wearing forms of misbehaviour.

Other misbehaviours that were identified by teachers in the survey during lessons – in descending order of frequency after the most common four examples already mentioned were:

- making unnecessary (non-verbal) noise (e.g. by scraping chairs, banging objects, moving clumsily)
- persistently infringing class (or school) rules (e.g. on dress, pupil behaviour)
- getting out of seat without permission
- verbal abuse towards other pupils (e.g. offensive or insulting remarks)
- general rowdiness, horseplay or mucking about
- cheeky or impertinent remarks or responses

- physical aggression towards other pupils (e.g. pushing, punching, striking)
- verbal abuse towards you (e.g. offensive, insulting, insolent or threatening remarks)
- physical destructiveness (e.g. breaking objects, damaging furniture and fabric)
- last on the list, as previously said, was, 'Physical aggression towards you (the teacher)'.

Before examining strategies for keeping disorderly conduct at bay or for laying it low when it occurs, it's important first to consider why misbehaviour arises in the first place.

Causes of misbehaviour

Some social scientists argue that student misbehaviour has less to do with the characteristics of students and more to do with the behaviour of teachers. Thus, for example, teachers who short-change on praise and go overboard on criticism increase the risk of serious confrontation with all students, even the usually well-behaved ones.

There is some truth in the assertion that teachers' actions can provoke disruptive incidents, but we do not believe this is the full story. Students can misbehave for all kinds of reasons, even in the classrooms of teachers whose own conduct is fair and reasonable. Perhaps before entering your classroom, a student has had a heated argument with another student. Sometimes these disputes will continue right through your lesson. Clearly, however, no blame can attach to you for why the matter erupted in the first place.

Whether student misbehaviour is linked to your actions or otherwise, it helps to know some of the more common reasons why students play up. That way, you will be better placed to engage in some preventive measures instead of waiting for trouble to start. Here is what students, who were involved in high-level disruptive incidents at the Cumbrian comprehensive school referred to earlier, told Bill Badger lay behind their behaviour. We have added some pre-emptive strike advice in brackets after each of the pre-determinants.

Teacher pre-determinants
- Teacher too soft. (Act as though you mean business.)
- Teacher too loud. (Lighten up.)

- Teacher not willing to listen. (Be a good listener.)
- Teacher simply a 'new one'. (Stay long enough to earn a reputation.)
- Teacher not even-handed. (Be fair and consistent.)

Lesson pre-determinants
- Lesson boring. (Liven things up.)
- Lesson theoretical, not practical. (Get down to earth.)

Student pre-determinants
- Student 'in a mood'. (Little preventive scope here, but be as conciliatory as is reasonable.)
- Student unable to do the work. (Set achievable tasks.)
- Student 'led on' by others. (A tricky one; an option is to identify and
  re-seat the ringleader/s.)
- Student affected by last lesson. (On a one-off basis, pre-emptive-
  strategies won't apply. If this happens regularly, talk to the teacher
  who takes the previous lesson with a view to removing the cause of
  the problem. Be diplomatic and don't impute blame to your colleague.)
- Student 'labelled'. (Tell the student nobody has a bad reputation in
  your class.)
- Student 'didn't realise'. ('That's all right, but here's how it needs to
  be in future'.)
- Student doing it 'for a laugh'. (Don't over-react if you're dealing
  with an attention-seeker.)

When Bill Badger got students aged 11–16 to write essays on both
teacher and student behaviour in the school, some interesting insights
emerged. For example, students reported that the following types of
teacher behaviour affected student or class behaviour (and here we
quote directly from the research):

- Teachers being late for lessons – a widespread comment from all
  years and all classes, seen in numerical terms as the commonest con-
  tributory factor to classroom disruption.
- Teachers being out of the room – also a widespread and common
  student perception as making a major contribution to classroom
  disruption.
- Teachers 'doing nothing' – a surprisingly repeated student comment
  across all years, the implication being that for the teacher not to act

on certain incidents increases the likelihood of their recurrence.

- Teachers being inconsistent – implying a failure of different teachers to uphold the same rules, and that individual teachers did not remain consistent over a period of time.
- Teachers being 'too soft', 'shouting too much' and 'not listening' were perceptions experienced through all years.

Here is some advice on how to prevent or respond to – as the case might be – these types of incident.

- Students have as much right as teachers to expect the respective parties to be punctual. Apart from the 'when the cats away, the mice will play' angle, being late means short-changing your students. So be punctual, and apologise if you're unavoidably delayed.
- Don't leave students unattended. Aside from the disruption that may arise, it's your job to teach and look after the students in your class. Their learning and their health and safety depend on your presence.
- Don't ignore unacceptable behaviour: not only will it stay, it'll come back with a vengeance. Make it clear that the misbehaviour isn't going to happen in your classroom: not now, not ever. Leave it at that. Dwelling on things, can make matters worse.
- Be consistent. Sudden mood changes confuse and disturb students. They like to know where you're coming from and where they're at. Admittedly, new teachers are still testing the water in terms of how they behave in front of students. That's fine. Just don't change gear too rapidly.
- Project confidence while still remaining fair-minded and kind, avoid any belligerence in the way you use your voice (apart from frightening some students, this can also invite hostile verbal retorts), and give students their fair say: they've got a right to be heard.

By now, we hope you've gathered that much disorderly conduct can be pre-emptively reduced by creating a school environment which students find interesting and relevant, and in which they don't get confused or upset by erratic swings of mood or aggressive behaviour on the part of teachers. Providing students with settings in which good behaviour thrives and effective learning flourishes has very little – if anything – to do with 'carrots and sticks'. It has much more to do with entitlement, with helping students get the education they deserve and not having to rely on the inducement of prizes (it's prize enough that they enjoy your lessons!) or the threat and use of punishment. But the DfE want you to know about rewards and sanctions. So we need to address those things. They exist in our school and in most schools.

We respond to the use of rewards and sanctions along broadly similar lines. Up until a couple of years ago, I used punishments lightly and sparingly. I still felt bad about doing that. Now, I don't use punishments at all. I'm not persuaded by their alleged efficacy, and I have ethical misgivings about giving students a hard time – even when they're making my life difficult! I'm convinced too that students work and behave better in non-coercive environments than they do in punitive regimes. As far as 'rewards' are concerned, I'm a little uncomfortable with that term. I believe that students deserve praise when they work hard, a supportive word in the ear when they're down, and a hot cup of coffee when we all need one, without all of this being defined in terms of recompense. I also believe that I don't have a discipline problem, despite working in a very big comprehensive school in a predominantly blue-collar neighbourhood. Such schools have a reputation (often undeservedly) of being tough.

But, like we said, rewards and sanctions are in the DfE criteria. So here goes.

Rewards and sanctions

'Cane-makers see bottom fall out of their market', proclaimed *The Observer*, in comical mood, on 1 May 1994. Coopers of Godalming, Surrey, Britain's oldest and biggest stick maker – suppliers of umbrellas and walking sticks to the landed gentry, and of canes to British schools for 150 years – do not plan to produce any more 'punishment canes'.

That decision makes good business sense: corporal punishment is no longer used in British state schools. Since its abolition, other ways of dealing with students who break the rules have been employed. High on the agenda, is reasoning with the misbehaving student outside the normal classroom setting. Sometimes this is done on a one-to-one basis, but it can also involve the participation of senior pastoral staff and of parents. Talking things through and arriving at mutually agreed upon conduct, is always a much better way to deal with discipline problems than resorting to punishment. Indeed, the Elton Report (1989) noted that, 'punitive regimes seem to be associated with worse rather than better standards of behaviour'. Before considering the use of sanctions in more detail, we'll look at the most effective way of keeping misbehaviour at bay: the promotion and rewarding of good behaviour and good work.

Promoting and rewarding good behaviour and good work

Schools that cultivate dialogue, engagement and mutual respect between students and staff, and which recognise and reward good behaviour and good work, do well on two important counts: they get less disruption and more learning.

Effective teachers promote and reward good behaviour and good work without resorting to 'get tough' tactics. They know that coercion creates an adversarial tension between students and teachers. They also know, as Chris Kyriacou (1993) points out that: 'If you convey to pupils that you are knowledgeable about the topic or subject, are interested in it, and can set up the learning activities skilfully, then pupils will respect your ability to teach; this will confirm your authority to manage their behaviour.'

It's very important to realise that the effective application of sound subject knowledge is, in itself, a powerful incentive to good student behaviour. Your professional standing as a teacher will rise if students sense that you know your subject and can present it in a way that engages and sustains their motivation. It's also important, for both behavioural and learning reasons, to give all students opportunities to succeed in your lessons. Doing a task well, confirms that a student has learnt how to do it. The accomplishment provides the student with an opportunity to gain enhanced self-esteem from being successful rather than from more dubious exploits, for example, the peer approval that sometimes derives from deviant antics.

Always reward success on task, and the good behaviour that invariably accompanies it, with appropriate praise. Don't be gushing though, and don't always be too public with your approbation. In classes where disruptive behaviour elicits peer approval (occasionally, the case among low achieving students – so make sure they do achieve!), over-indulgent teacher praise can embitter students who normally get their kudos from being rebellious.

When about nine hundred secondary school students in the West Midlands were asked, during a survey, which reward for good behaviour or sound work they valued most, they rated a letter home very highly indeed (Wheldall and Merrett 1988, cited in the Elton Report). It's always sensible to heed what students say on these matters. So make sure that complimentary messages home feature prominently in the rewards you issue.

Some other tried and tested rewards that you can incorporate into your class-management portfolio are set out below.

- Good comments entered in exercise books for effort and achievement. Don't restrict things to the unimaginative, 'Well done'. If a piece of work deserves an accolade, be generous with your compliments. Here's an example of what we have in mind: 'You've put a great deal of effort into this assignment Sharif. I was very impressed with the report on your visit to the Viking Museum. The vivid way in which you write about the sights, sounds and smells of the re-constructed Viking village jump right off the pages. Your impressive research and excellent work have earned you an "A".'
- If your school provides students with work record books for comments by teachers on behaviour, effort and achievement (usually read and signed by parents on a weekly basis), communicate your praise whenever appropriate. Positive remarks in these books enhance the self-esteem of students, and reduce the incidence of anti-school sentiments (often prompted by negative labelling).
- Show your students that you value their accomplishments by displaying their work prominently in classrooms, corridors and entrance foyers. To avoid making some students feel left out, include collaborative work in displays.
- Use assemblies to commend and endorse good behaviour, vigorous effort and worthy achievements. Public praise engenders collective goodwill.
- Give your students occasional treats without the need for them to feel they have had to earn them. Here are a few of our treats: sending them postcards when we're on holiday, form-time breakfasts, and end of term class parties.
- Take students to one side and warmly congratulate genuine effort and real achievement. Personal praise works wonders in the building of non-coercive relationships between teachers and students. It is also a powerful disincentive to the formation of disruptive, student subcultures.

It is a good idea to involve students in the discussion of acceptable codes of conduct, and to encourage them to take some ownership of the rules and rewards that support good behaviour and genuine effort. Non-adversarial dialogue of this sort, is much better than coercive, 'Do-what-I-say' regimes. If we can't persuade students – without cajoling and threatening them – to behave well and work hard, we'll never get the best out of them. The majority of students will do what they're told if threatened with punishment. However, they'll resent the threat, and will tend to do the bare minimum of what's demanded. By contrast, praise at task and open discussion about reasonable rules when students are in good order, reduce the risk of them losing interest in what they're doing and messing around on other occasions.

There are still times, however, when probably most teachers resort to punishment.

Punishments

Schools use punishments to signal serious disapproval of student behaviours that breach clearly defined boundaries of acceptable conduct. In that context, 'the use of punishment is intended to help the pupil appreciate the gravity and seriousness with which you are treating the misbehaviour and the urgency of the need for acceptable behaviour to occur in future' (Chris Kyriacou, 1993).

If you decide to punish students, it's imperative that you make it clear to them beforehand what kinds of conduct constitute punishable offences. Most students respect fair play, and they respond better to 'just' and consistently applied punishments for misbehaviour than they do to unreasonable and arbitrary 'sharp shocks'.

Rules, however, mustn't be enforced with the formulaic dogma that applies a rigid scale of punishments to every definable offence. For example, a student who deliberately skips a lesson, might be told that she or he has broken a serious rule for which a detention would normally be imposed. It's up to the teacher though to determine whether a punishment is appropriate in this case. If the student didn't turn up through fear of being taunted by a bully in the class, counselling would be a far more effective and a more just strategy than a detention. It's also very important not to punish legitimate student protests or out-of-character outbursts. Learn to distinguish between open defiance to reasonable authority, dissent based on sincere conviction, and flash point outbursts linked to personal troubles.

Allowing for the fact that some offences – however serious – require non-punitive responses, when punishments are deployed, the severity of the sanction is usually linked to the gravity of the bad conduct. Here, on an approximately rising scale of harshness, follow some of the more commonly used punishments in secondary schools.

- A disapproving glance. Surprisingly effective, this strategy is often used in the following manner: teacher stops talking, pauses and looks at the student to bring her or him to order. It works nearly every time without the need for further action. While still maintaining eye contact, add a quick smile when the student has come to order. It concludes the matter amicably.
- A 'ticking-off'. This technique, otherwise referred to as a mild reprimand, is best employed by taking the student to one side after a lesson. The aim of the ticking-off, is to make the student aware that a rule has been broken and to register your disapproval. It should be accompanied with a clear statement from you that the rule-breaking behaviour should not be repeated. Some teachers add an 'or else' proviso here, indicating the exact nature of the sanction that will follow if the misbehaviour re-occurs.

  There are times when you might judge it appropriate to deliver a public reprimand during a lesson, for example, when a student's behaviour is seriously disruptive. The same principles apply as before. Be especially careful to direct your reprimand against the offending behaviour, not against the individual student. Far better to say, 'The protective goggles are designed to be worn, not to be thrown across the science laboratory', than, 'Stop acting like a two-year old with those goggles'. Public reprimands should never humiliate or insult a student. That's unethical; it's also likely to provoke a hostile response. On the other hand, when a teacher firmly but fairly criticises a student's misbehaviour in front of the whole class, it can have a ripple effect by preventing similar antics occurring among other students.
- Setting of tasks. This can vary from lines (a bit old-fashioned these days, as well as having zero educational value) to written accounts of why the student should not misbehave. The punishment is usually reserved for petty offences, for example, not handing in homework on the due date.
- Negative comments in work record books (where this system is used). This brings the proscribed behaviour of the student to the

attention of other interested parties (notably, parents and senior teachers) who usually monitor these books. The comments should aim to correct the identified misbehaviour. Here's an example: 'Julie will make much better progress in French when she stops chatting with other students during lessons'.

- Detentions. For minor misdemeanours (for example, queue jumping in the dinner line) the detention is given during school breaks. The after-school detention is usually reserved for more serious offences (for example, repeated lateness to morning registration without reasonable excuse). It's a double-edged sword because it involves a prior notice communication with parents, as well as the inconvenience to the student of being detained outside of normal school hours.

- Privilege withdrawals. The privileges removed include: non-participation in favoured classroom activities (for example, playing the drums in a music lesson), and exclusion from school outings (for example, a geography field trip). The punishment might fit the crime, by being imposed for improper conduct which has occurred during a privileged activity.

- Referring the student to a senior colleague, for example, a head of department or a head of year. This strategy should be avoided for minor matters because it sends a message to the student that you can't handle the situation on your own. In that respect, it can be damaging to the authority that you convey as a teacher. Referrals are typically used when repeated alternative measures to remedy the unacceptable conduct have been tried by a teacher without any significant success. Examples of offences for which this strategy might be used include: serious disruptive behaviour during lessons, gross insubordination to a teacher, and truancy (even first time offences, with this one).

- Placing on report. This is a fairly serious form of referral. It invariably involves bringing to the attention of senior colleagues the targeted misconduct, and formalising matters by monitoring the behaviour of the student over a set period, perhaps a week or so. During the agreed period, the student carries a report card into each lesson (and sometimes into form registrations), which is completed and signed by individual teachers for each session. Teachers write their comments about the conduct of the student on the report card. They might be asked to consider the censured behaviour when they

111

make their observations. For example, in the case of a student who is on report for swearing at a member of staff (a very rare offence), the teacher might write, 'Ian conducted himself courteously at all times in his dealings with me'. If agreed by senior staff, the report card can be sent home for the signature of parents. Home referrals are very unpopular with students, and they thus significantly add to the severity of the punishment.

- Temporary exclusion from the classroom. This tends to be used when the misbehaviour of a student makes it very difficult for a teacher to conduct a lesson. If, for example, a student constantly refuses to follow reasonable instructions to get on with work and to stop distracting other students by shouting across the classroom, it becomes virtually impossible for the lesson to proceed. In these circumstances, a teacher might arrange for the student to work independently under the eye of a duty teacher, typically, a senior member of staff. Some schools have withdrawal units with attending supervisory staff for students who are temporarily excluded from the classroom. Periods of exclusion can vary from one single lesson on a particular day to every lesson for up to a week or more. Students are returned to the classroom once it's decided that they're ready to resume the normal routine. A letter home to parents (usually from the student's form tutor or a senior teacher) informing them of the seriousness of their child's misbehaviour and of the steps taken by the school to deal with it, strengthens the impact of the punishment.

- Exclusion from school. This can be temporary or permanent. It is reserved for very serious misbehaviour, for example, assaulting another student or a member of staff, malicious damage to school property, distributing drugs on school premises, serious bullying, repeatedly breaking school rules etc. Exclusion is an end-of-the-line, final resort punishment. It's customarily administered by the most senior member of staff, the headteacher, to whose attention the misbehaviour will have been referred. All exclusions involve communication between the school and the home. In the case of temporary exclusion, parents will be asked to take responsibility for their daughter or son during school hours, and they'll be advised that reinstatement will only occur once it's judged that the excluded student is ready to comply with the school code of conduct. With this end in mind, the school might draw up a behaviour contract for the student to sign before returning to school. Permanent exclusion is a very rare step, normally reserved for the most incorrigible and persistent forms of misbehaviour. Permanently excluded students can seek admission to another school.

A survey published in *The Times Educational Supplement* (21 January, 1994) of the headteachers of nearly one hundred schools in England and Wales, found that the most common punishment in secondary schools was detention. Primary schools favoured removal of privileges or letters home to parents. Most schools said they would suspend a student for violence or bullying, making this permanent if the banned behaviour persisted. Drug pushers would be expelled by all the headteachers who participated in the survey. However, a significant minority said they wouldn't expel a student for possession or taking of drugs, but would approach outside agencies to provide counselling. Most headteachers reported they would suspend or expel students for theft or vandalism. More than one in nine secondary schools, had permanently excluded at least one student in the last year – arson, drugs and violence figured in some of these cases. One in three primary schools, had suspended a student during recent years, and one in six, had used permanent exclusions.

If you do decide to punish students, here are some very important cautionary guidelines.

Things you must never do
- Use corporal punishment. It's against the law and it's likely to provoke a very aggressive response from students. Don't even place your hand on a student's shoulder during a reprimand, or if the 'offender' walks away from you. Doing that, without the student's consent (which clearly won't be given) constitutes an assault in law.
- Get personal. Criticise the offending behaviour, but don't insult the culprit. Slighting students, especially when they have a reputation to defend in the presence of peers, is one of the quickest ways we know of inviting an immediate and an ugly confrontation.
- Use sarcasm or any other humiliating tactics. Such conduct is deeply resented by students. You'll never earn their respect if you ridicule them, but you will become a rapidly unpopular teacher.
- Lose your cool. Don't shout at students or vent hostile displays of anger. Such behaviour can frighten some students, and can lead to

113

retaliatory verbal outbursts from others. Teachers who lack self-control are sometimes feared but never respected.

- Make threats (actual or idle). Threatening students is an inappropriate way to deal with people. Moreover, if the threat is unrealistic ('I'm keeping the whole class in for an hour every day next week if one more student talks out of turn') or not followed through ('I know I said I'd give you lines if you did that again, but I'm going to let you off'), your credibility will diminish.
- Be inconsistent. Arbitrary punishments that don't fit the gravity of the offence or which are not administered even-handedly, provoke strong antipathy among students.
- Push things too far. Once you've made your point, leave it at that. Over-reacting and imposing excessive sanctions can lead to heated exchanges.
- Punish the whole class. Guaranteed to alienate up to thirty odd students (including the righteously indignant innocent) at a stroke, this is also likely to prompt understandable protest from some parents.

We don't want to end this chapter by dwelling on the sanctions component of the DfE Class Management Competence. Punishments are last resort tactics, and, if used injudiciously, they cause more problems than they solve. Our professional experience, and the findings of recent research, show that the most effective class managers are teachers who manage their students' behaviour and learning without coercion. These are the teachers who motivate students instead of pushing them around, the teachers who hit all the 'feel-good' buttons rather than forcing unwilling and resented conformity. Class management works best in an atmosphere distinguished by its civility and generosity of spirit. We urge you to make the creation of such an atmosphere a paramount aim of your professional practice.

We think it's also vital to emphasise the importance of having and conveying a sense of humour in your work with students. Newly qualified teachers are sometimes unsure about the extent to which it's safe to use humour without compromising their authority. On the contrary, provided your humour isn't sarcastic, racist, sexist or any other way designed to humiliate, it'll help you to gain a good rapport with your students, as well as enhancing your status in their eyes. That's as long as the humour doesn't become too matey or over-indulgent. In those cases, you'll run the risk of losing the respect that your office carries.

Used sensibly, humour can also be an excellent device for dealing with certain types of improper conduct. Here are a few examples.

- Student resting face-down against the desk.
  Teacher: 'Are you still listening for the galloping of hooves in the distance, Andrew?'
- Student failing to hand in an assignment on the due date, apparently through forgetfulness (a common excuse).
  Teacher: 'There's only room enough for one absent-minded professor in this class, and that's me.'
- Student eating in class.
  Teacher: (after gaining eye contact with the student in question) 'I was thinking of eating my sandwiches during the lesson, but people tell me I'm a terrible slurper.'

Note that in all the above examples, the teacher avoids making any personally offensive remarks. Instead, it's the teacher who tends to employ mildly, self-deprecating asides, while simultaneously and humorously getting over a point.

Provided it is used sensibly and in good taste, humour should be a key feature of your class-management style. If you already have a well-developed sense of humour, you will go far. If not, without being unduly artificial, lighten up a bit, smile more often, and, as appropriate, share a joke with your students when you all find something to laugh about.

What your mentor should do for you

Effective class managers create achievable, stimulating learning environments, and they get the best from their students, in terms of behaviour and learning. While effective class management can't be pinned down to one specific quality, best practice invariably involves: getting to know the individually, preferred learning styles of students, their different kinds of intelligence, and the tasks that grab their interest and – through being achievable but stretching – promote their self-esteem. Observe how effective teachers acquire that valuable knowledge, and how they act on it; then imitate those best practices that fit your own style and temperament.

115

OBSERVATION

Arrangements should be made for you to observe the activities listed below.

- Whole-class, group and individual teaching. Ask your mentor to provide opportunities to watch teachers whose style is particularly geared to one of these methods. Expect to find, for example, quite a lot of whole-class teaching from mathematics and science teachers, a fair amount of group work from performing arts and PE teachers, and a reasonable extent of individual teaching from special needs teachers. Make a point of watching the teachers who mix and match these different methods to good effect.

- Lessons by teachers who have a reputation (particularly, among their students) for making learning lots of fun. Every mentor will know who these stars are. Yet, sadly, too few practising teachers get to watch their most successful colleagues making even the seemingly dull topics lively, the normally remote issues relevant, and the most complex problems understandable. Make sure you don't miss out here.

- Lessons and recess duties by teachers who are known to be respected by students, yet whose approach ranges from 'strict disciplinarian' to 'easy-going coaxer'. These teachers seem to get it just right, whatever their style, with even the most recalcitrant students. Watch them in action, especially in potential 'flash-point areas', like: science laboratories, dining halls, playgrounds, corridors and bus bay areas, and try to figure out what they've got that commands respect – but not fear. Despite their differences in approach, these teachers typically have forceful personalities, an impeccable sense of fairness, a feisty sense of humour, a confident and robust presence, and an uncanny ability to convey these attractive qualities in their dealings with people around them. Ask them what their secret is – we'd like to know!

PRACTICE

Get your mentor to provide you with hands-on experience in the activities listed below.

- Giving whole-class lectures (for example, the origins of slavery), whole-class explanations (for example, how to work out percentages) and the supervision of whole-class exercises (for example, monitoring a written comprehension in which all the students are involved). Whole-class teaching will sharpen your voice register and will enhance your confidence.

• Setting up, co-ordinating and supporting group and individual work (for example, scripted role play in performing arts, and individual instruction of students who have special needs). These methods are great for getting to know students on a 'person' basis. You'll be a better teacher for that.

• Conducting recess, school dinner and other similar supervisory duties. Students are more likely to be less restrained, for better or worse, when they're outside of classrooms. Now is the time to talk to them about their favourite bands and sports teams, as well as keeping them gently in check if they get too boisterous. Do plenty of shadowing of experienced teachers before going solo with any of these duties. Also, remember what we said earlier: try to avoid public rebuking of students who might be misbehaving when they're in the company of their peers. One of my favourite approaches to dealing with disruptive antics in corridors and other public areas is to say, confidently, quite loudly and with a friendly smile: 'Come on now ladies and gentlemen, take it easy, calm down!' It rarely fails, and it seldom provokes an angry backlash because it's not a personal rebuke.

• Doing some substitute teaching. This is a great way of learning to think on your feet and to react to the unpredictable. Ask any experienced teacher what they find most demanding from a 'maintaining order' point of view, and most of them will tell you it's substituting a Year 9, 10 or 11 class in a subject area outside the teacher's own, where the absent teacher has forgotten to leave set work, and it's a Friday afternoon.

A 'pre- emptive-strike' strategy that might avoid you ending up in this situation in the first place, is to ask the head of department of the absent teacher what arrangements have been made for the lesson you'll be substituting. This will usually ensure, if prior provision hasn't been made, that all the students know what to do and have the necessary books and other equipment to get on with the assigned task. If that fails, improvisation is called for. Here are a couple of useful ploys: have a substitute teacher's 'survival pack' close to hand at all times (these can be purchased or custom-made by you – they include word and number games, quizzes and puzzles); tell the class they can get on with any work, including homework.

Action points

1 Adopt a flexible strategy to whole-class, group and one-to-one teaching. Mix and match these options to create a stimulating learning environment, as well as one in which teaching style is linked to learning need.

2 Never lecture for more than twenty minutes if you intend to keep the attention of your students.

3 Re-arrange the furniture. Rows of desks might be suitable for 'chalk and talk', but a 'boardroom' table of re-arranged desks, is excellent for class discussion. Remember that students should not actually move furniture themselves, unless the school's Code of Practice on Health and Safety allows this.

4 Foster a task-oriented atmosphere, which achieves its orderliness through motivating students rather than by threatening them with punishment.

5 Cut a bold but non-threatening presence with your class by cultivating withitness and a confident, unflustered manner.

6 Accept that the best reward you can give your students is to make their learning fun, as well as achievable, and act on that understanding.

7 Become acquainted with the rewards and sanctions system in the school where you work, and don't rock the boat too much. That said, put justice before any institutional 'cheap shots'.

8 Use praise often, and punishment (if you decide to use it) sparingly, consistently and in measured doses.

9 Inject some humour, without being unduly jolly, into your relationship with students. They'll appreciate you for it, and you'll make significant headway in creating a warm, friendly learning environment.

CHAPTER 5

Assessment
and recording

'Have you marked my book yet Miss?'
'Why has Samantha got a higher mark than me?'
'Don't you remember, I put my book on your desk, last week?'
'What does my child need to do to get better marks?'

In some ways, assessment is the very stuff of the teacher's job. Not because it grades, stratifies and positions students, but because it's the background and the indicator against which you – and, increasingly, the Government – assess your personal effectiveness. It's the measure of your knowledge of your students and the information you feed into your planning. You can't possibly decide what to teach, unless you know where your students are now. You can't possibly decide what level to pitch your lessons at, unless you know what your students are expecting from you, what they're used to.

The DfE (1992) expects teachers to assess and record the progress of students. It has prescribed this principle as follows.

2.5 Newly qualified teachers should be able to:

2.5.1 identify the current level of attainment of individual pupils using NCATs, statements of attainment and end of key stage statements where applicable

2.5.2 judge how well each pupil performs against the standard expected of a pupil of that age

2.5.3 assess and record systematically the progress of individual pupils

2.5.4 use such assessment in their teaching

2.5.5 demonstrate that they understand the importance of reporting to pupils on their progress and of marking their work regularly against agreed criteria.

Putting this into more concise terms, Assessment and Recording of Pupils' Progress, as defined by the DfE, refers to: the ability to use NCATs and other criteria; to judge accurately the performance of students, taking into account their age; to record this information efficiently and clearly; to feed it back into teaching; and to make this assessment process clear to the students.

Assessment and recording has always been important to teachers. In the past, though, teachers tended to carry lots of information in their heads. Rightly or wrongly, this teacher-centred assessment has been largely dismantled, and replaced with a much more public system of assessment and recording. In its favour, this does de-mystify the process, and makes it easier, for parents and students alike, to get access to the processes by which they're educationally judged. Against it is the increased amount of time that has to be spent talking or writing about a student rather than teaching or preparing to teach that student. What is clearly necessary is a way to fulfil assessment and recording criteria quickly and efficiently and within the normal teaching process as far as possible.

We'll begin by looking at the process of assessing students against formal criteria.

Identifying the current level of attainment

(See update on page viii)
DfE criterion 2.5.1 states that newly qualified teachers should be able to identify the current Level of Attainment of individual students using NCATs, Statements of Attainment and end of Key Stage statements

where applicable. It doesn't matter whether you teach a core curriculum subject or not, you'll be required to carry out some form of assessment against formal written criteria. It could be against examination board level descriptors (normally a paragraph outlining the basic qualities associated with a particular grade) or your school's own Scheme of Work for Personal and Social Education. But most of you will be assessing in the core curriculum subjects, where you'll be expected to use the National Curriculum Statements of Attainment relating to the ten-point scale (retained, under scrutiny, in the Final Dearing Report, December 1993). This is a scale of assessment where 1 is the lowest and 10 is the highest. These levels are expressed in terms of letter grades in Key Stage 4 GCSE results. This whole area is under review at present, but there seems to be considerable support for the retention of the ten-point scale, at least at Key Stages 1, 2 and 3.

In theory, the ten-level assessment ought to be easy to do; there you have them, the Statements of Attainment in black and white; all you have to do is read them and see if they apply to your student's piece of work. But it is not quite that simple. Let us quote from English in the National Curriculum (the English Orders), Attainment Target 3 (En3 – Writing), Level 5, Strand C: 'Pupils should be able to demonstrate increased effectiveness in the use of standard English (except in contexts where non-standard forms are needed for literary purposes) and show an increased differentiation between speech and writing.'

Although English has particular problems of its own because it's a more skills-based rather than a content-based subject, the problems inherent in the whole formation of the Statements of Attainment are quite apparent in this example. The first and most obvious of these, is that the Statements of Attainment in all the subjects are clearly meant to be used at the end of a Key Stage, or at least on a range of work. You, as a teacher, will normally be assessing individual pieces of work as part of the continuous process of assessment. How can you demonstrate increased effectiveness without any other work to refer them to? There's no point pretending; this is a problem. There isn't nearly enough support in the National Curriculum documents for the assessing of individual pieces of work. Clearly, you can't leave all assessment until the end of the Key Stage or until your students have amassed a body of work. Ideally, they need feedback after each piece of work, and you need this information to help your planning and interim reporting. How can this be resolved?

We think there are two stages to resolving the issue. The first is to determine the general Level of Attainment that the student at that stage should be achieving. The expected Level of Attainment and the appropriate Key Stage should be listed in DfE documents. Ask your head of department for these, or there may be a special person in charge of assessment that you'll need to see. With any luck, your department will have its own established policy, perhaps as part of a departmental hand-book. As far as we're aware, the Level/Key Stage relationship that was set out in DES (as the DfE was previously known) Circular No. 2/90 still holds, and that is:

Key Stage	*Levels*
KS1	1–3
KS2	2–5
KS3	3–8
KS4	3–10

As you can see, there's some overlap between Key Stages, but at least when you're confronted with a pile of work from Year 9 students, you'll know that you should (there's no guarantee though) have work that falls between Level 3 and Level 8. This, at least, gives you some guidance as to what Levels to expect to be awarding. Once you've ascertained this, you need to put students' work into rank order, basically, on gut instinct (more about that attribute in the final section of this chapter). Once you've got your top and bottom candidates, you'll need to attempt to assess these as firmly as possible against relevant Statements of Attainment. When you've assessed them, the other candidates will fall into place more easily, relative to their, by now, assessed peers.

We've said very glibly above, attempt to assess these as firmly as possible. This is easier said than done. The Statements of Attainment are riddled with words and phrases like – increased, confidently, effectively and show awareness of. These are qualitative terms that can't be interpreted in any binding way. When I first began to assess work using the new Statements of Attainments, I suffered from that well-known teachers' disease – rabbit in the headlights syndrome. So much new information seemed to be bearing down on me that I lost the will to act. In addition, my security had been taken away, in terms of the old grading system (fortunately, as a new teacher, you won't suffer from this), and, as a result, I tended to fasten on to the Statements of

122

Attainment in a literal and legalistic way. The language they are written in is too bland to support this kind of interpretation, so rather than try and pin your students down to individual phrases, clauses and words in the Statements of Attainment, read them to assess their overall sense, and then determine if the students fall within the general compass of them. Take their vagueness as a freedom, and assess in their general spirit.

This works in practice. At agreement trials I've attended (occasions when teachers and examiners get together to assess standard material to bring their marking into line with the official standards), wherever teachers have marked legalistically, trying to make each candidate address every part of a Statement of Attainment, their marks have been one or two levels below the grade finally awarded to the candidate. I rest my case.

Some cause for comfort (in one sense, anyway), is that many subjects are assessed totally or mainly by terminal or end of module examinations or tests. These, of course, however, or by whom, they are marked (a cause of some dispute at the moment), will very likely be externally moderated (that is, checked and adjusted by examiners from outside the school), and will, if you mark them, probably be assessed against a mark-scheme (instructions that tell you how to assess an examination or test paper). This, in a sense, takes the pressure off you in terms of a binding final assessment, but it keeps the pressure on with regard to feeding back to the students their performance, as well as predicting for them, their parents and the school, their likely overall assessment.

Age-related assessment

DfE criterion 2.5.2 says that newly qualified teachers should be able to judge how well each student performs against the standard expected of a student of that age.

As we've said above, you do have some guidance as to what range of Levels to expect from each Key Stage. That said, Key Stages don't directly relate to ages of students. Key Stage 3, for example, encompasses students aged 11–14. So how can you tell if a student is performing at the Level expected for someone of a specified age? Behind this question, lurks all kinds of implications about the nature of child development and the role of schools should play in this.

We believe that there's an extreme and slightly distorted Piagetian view at work here. This view is a notion, based on the ideas of the zoologist and psychologist, Jean Piaget (1896–1980), that children develop through certain stages at a certain time in their life, and that – give or take a sparse dispersal above and below the average child – most 12-year olds should be at a certain level of attainment. Obviously, people who hold this view haven't been in a classroom too often. For classrooms are full of people with diverse backgrounds, experiences, talents and dispositions. To look for a standard to be apparent in a class of Year 7 students, in their behaviour and in their work, is as meaningful as looking for a standard in height, shoe size or hair colour.

So how can we make sense of the DfE age-related assessment criterion? We think you need to dispose of the whole notion of a standard expected of a student of a particular age, as if it's something given, and look to your Programmes of Study and your Attainment Targets, and then pose the question: 'What do the students need to be able to do to be successful and happy for their year group?' This simplifies everything. Gone are any woolly conceptions as to what students of particular ages should be able to do – a passive assessment process. Instead, you decide, after consulting appropriate colleagues and documentation, what you want them to be able to do – an active process. The next step is plain: set diagnostic work to find out what the students can already do, speak to them to find out what they already know, then design your course around the results of this, if need be, setting individualised work to fill any gaps or weaknesses. This way, you're addressing your teaching to real students, not a notional standard (see Chapter 3, for details of planning and student consultation).

Assessing and recording the progress of individual students

DfE criterion 2.5.3 lays down that newly qualified teachers should be able to assess and record systematically the progress of individual students. We've already said a little about doing this in Chapter 3. As we said there, this can be a very onerous task, and one that can occupy huge amounts of time to very little effect, if it's not done as part of your normal teaching process, and if the records you keep are not easily usable thereafter. Make sure your basic records for each student are simple, detailed and all in one place (as far is allowable, under examination board and government regulations). If you can record all you need to on a couple of pages of a mark-book, then this is the best possible solution. We'll now discuss mark-book formats.

There are as many different ways of setting out a mark-book as there are teachers marking. Personally, I have five pages per class: one for attendance, one for oral marks, one for written marks, one for a diagnostic skills breakdown, and one for miscellaneous items, like books borrowed, money owed etc. You may need more pages, depending on your subject. I'll now go through the layout of the different pages.

1 The attendance register is simply a class list of students, alphabetically by surname (always with their first name written first). I always leave an extra column to record the students' preferred version of their names, for example, Si for Simon. You'd be surprised how much this tiny courtesy can improve your relationships with the students. I write down the number of students in that particular class somewhere on the page – you'll often need to know this figure for stock ordering, resource booking and allocating students for group work. It helps if the page of your mark-book is squared. To mark attendance, simply put a / in a square, and, for the next attendance, put a \, so together they look like /\. This makes attendances quick to count up. For absent, put O and for late, L. For any of the other myriad reasons for non-attendance, for example, extra music or Spanish lessons, use the symbols your school has adopted.The diagram below will clarify things for you.

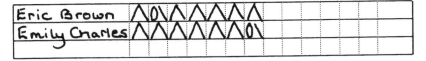

2 & 3 The pages for oral marks and written marks are roughly the same. I cut them lengthwise, about 5cm from the page edge, so the list of names can be seen from the attendance page when these other pages are folded over. At the top of the page, I write down the date of the assessment, the name of the assessment work and the assignment number (this is a unique number, normally a combination of group or teacher initials and a sequence number, that can identify a piece of work for examination or assessment purposes, for example,

HS3), where relevant. I write these lengthwise down the page, so that the mark only needs to take up one column. Underneath these headings, I write the relevant mark, level with the name of the appropriate student.

4 The diagnostic skills breakdown is, for me, the most important part of my recording and assessment. It's what defines my approach to each individual student. Marks and grades, although based on an informed view at the time of marking, don't really represent useful information. At the time of marking, you'll have based your assessment on an audit of different skills and qualities, as represented in the written work or presentation. However, later on, you'll, unless you're a person of incredible memory, have forgotten what that audit took account of. If asked to give advice, to consult with a parent or student or write a report, you'll be very hard pressed to produce sufficiently detailed information from grades alone. What I have found extremely useful in this respect, is to record the actual things that made me assess in the way I did. This sounds a weighty task but it isn't. All you need to do, is to work out what are the fundamental skills in your subject area. For example, in English, fundamental skills include sentence punctuation, paragraphing, apostrophes etc. You can break down these skills as much as you like, but what you need to do, is to array symbols for the skills (how you symbolise them is up to you, but keep it simple; for example, my symbol for the use of commas is simply a ',') across the top of the page. Alongside each student's name, under the appropriate symbol, put a tick if they're good at it, a cross if they're not. (See the example below.)

		,	•	ẞ/ẞ	Voc.	Spelling	Pres.						
Eric Brown		✓	✓	✓	✗	✗	✗						
Emily Charles		✗	✓	✗	✓	✓	✓						

You can use this information to target the student, assess the need for whole group teaching in certain areas (for example, if the students all can't use speech punctuation), to talk knowledgeably about individual students at parents' evenings, and to write personalised, relevant reports. You can also, if you like, record things like lateness of handing in work and any attitude problems here.

5 My miscellaneous page is surprisingly useful. It helps me keep a handle on the 'general purpose administration' that needs to be recorded on each student in a particular class. It's largely a 'tick boxes affair': did Sally do her oral presentation today? A tick against her name means, yes. A red circle, denotes that Sally was absent, so I'd better catch her next time.

A few concluding remarks about assessing and recording. Your school may have a recording system of its own that you might have to use. Moreover, certain guidelines about what has to be recorded, have to be adhered to regarding examination and National Curriculum work, which may compromise your system. What we advise, however, is that you stick to two following basic principles.

1 Don't record unnecessary information.
2 Try to centralise your information storage, so it's accessible and easy to up-date.

One final word of warning: it is still the case that teachers are not supposed to report National Curriculum Levels at any time other than at the end of the Key Stage. Before sharing your assessments with students or writing them on work, find out what your school's policy is on this issue. Some schools and departments are against issuing marks on principle, on the grounds that it de-motivates the less able. You must find out what this policy is in your particular school, as a matter of urgency.

Using assessment in your teaching

DfE criterion 2.5.4 specifies that *newly qualified teachers should be able to* use such assessment as they make (my italics) in their teaching.

Marking and grading, in themselves, are not useful to students. Grades are just labels applied to them, which, if you're lucky, they think have been allocated fairly and evenly by you. If your relationship with the class isn't too good, the students may think that the grades are allocated according to your mood and what esteem you hold them in currently. Here, assessment becomes a personal issue.

This is to be avoided at all costs; all kinds of resentments and misunderstandings can arise. It's in your best interest and that of the students, for you to make clear exactly what criteria you're marking against, that the machinery the students are being judged by, is bigger than both of you. This depersonalises the process of judgement and gives you a common cause, an important relationship-building tool. I regularly say to students things like, 'Great piece of writing! Lively, vivid, good use of unusual vocabulary But until you begin to use paragraphs, I'm afraid I can't award you more than a ....' This makes the mark or grade understandable. I've given feedback on the parts of the assignment that were good, and set a target that will ensure enhanced results in the future. The same process should be applied to written comments.

To sum up, always find something good to say, always comment on the parts of the work that were effective, whether they contributed to the final grade or not. Always explain your marks, and always set concrete targets for the next piece of work (actually, it's probably better if you set one important target, rather than a few).

One simple way to ensure that individual students are heeding your advice, is to flip back to previous targets in their work, when marking the current piece. If they're not, then you're quite justified in asking them if they require further assistance. If the answer is, 'No', then you say, 'My hands are tied!' and deny them a higher grade. This puts the ball firmly back in their court, where it has to be if they are to progress. One note of caution though, if you're going to be as 'hawkish' as this, you need to be absolutely sure that they do know what they're doing. Many people say yes when they mean no, to protect their ego. If students say they understand a target skill, I always ask them to explain it to me. This has the following important advantages.

1 It makes sure advice goes to the right students.
2 It reinforces the students' grasp of the skill. Often explaining aloud to others, improves our own understanding (it elaborates the memory trace with auditory information that can be used as cues, as cognitive psychologists would say).

To conclude, marking and assessment should be seen as inevitable and integral to the teaching process, not something arbitrary and personally judgemental. The way to achieve this is to make the criteria clear, the source of the criteria known and the application of them

128

explicit. It's important that you follow up any advice given on an individual level because students, being people, will only do what they have to do! Just like us!

Reporting on progress

DfE criterion 2.5.5 says that newly qualified teachers should be able to demonstrate that they understand the importance of reporting to students on their progress and of marking their work regularly against agreed criteria.

We've covered most of this competence in the previous section, at least as far as the teacher/student/assessment relationship is concerned. However, the use of the word reporting, reminds us that the other half of the recording and assessment of students' progress is the public one of formally issuing reports to students and their parents or guardians.

My reports from school were one-line indictments. One example from an English teacher said: 'Crawley clearly has intelligence but his handwriting is abominable. Could do better. C+' Apart from the bitterness I still feel for being chewed up and spat out in such a terse fashion, this report really doesn't give any advice or assessment of skills. In general, teachers can no longer get away with such reports. In fact, the whole area of reporting is in flux, lurching towards some kind of reviewing process, where the student contributes to the document and sometimes even the parent too. People bandy phrases around like: formative assessment (assessing the student while working – the processes involved in education), summative assessment (the grading at a particular end point) and Records of Achievement, or ROAs as they are more commonly known (an example of summative assessment in a neatly bound document wallet). You'll often hear these three letters spat out with venom, sometimes coupled with the phrase, 'Waste of time!' or worse. While the move towards more participatory formative assessment should be welcomed, it isn't working very well at present because of muddled thinking and under-resourcing.

One of my favourite quotes comes from Mark Twain, who said, 'When some people discharge an obligation, you can hear the report from miles around.' This, I think, sums up exactly where reporting in education is now. There is too much emphasis on the final quality and finish of the reporting document and not enough on the benefits to students and parents of it. I welcome the opportunity to introduce formative assessment in the form of student comments on reports and review sheets and ROAs. The students are the important part of the process and should be allowed to comment on it, and teachers should be able to comment on students' comments. But for this to be worthwhile, it must become part of the everyday classroom activities, not something done only at report time. There is no point consulting a student on formative issues that have taken place over a whole year, just at the end of the year. If you do, what they'll produce for you, will be informal and, in effect, summative, but written in the language of formative. They may even produce total fiction to fill up the space on the review sheet. In short, it would be waste of time. If you believe in this kind of reporting, you must make it part of your general working practice. Otherwise, it's an empty exercise.

Given what I've said above, you need to make sure you know your school's policy on reporting and follow it. It may be that the school has opted for a minimal model of reporting, reminiscent of my one-liner above. Some schools opt for computer-generated reports, in which case all you do is feed in numbers or pencilled sheets. If the school has chosen the fuller review model (possibly, a sheet of A4, with sections for you, the student and parents to write in), you'll have a lot of writing (or word-processing) ahead of you.

In that case, it will seem more worthwhile if you avoid being bland, so use the records you've kept to really inform your writing. Make sure your reports are individual for each student, even if they are all quite similar people in terms of personality and ability. Nobody likes to feel the same as anybody else, and students usually compare notes. Try to avoid the most awful reporting situation that you can have when you mix two (or more) of the more reticent students up with each other. Always in a class, there will be strong, memorable characters (both for good reasons and bad), but there will also be a coterie of less noticeable students.

While it's your job to get to know everybody in your classes, it can happen, with the numbers passing through your hands, that you get confused about students. One simple way to avoid this, is to ask all your new students at the beginning of a year, to bring in a passport photograph of themselves, which is affixed to the front of their exercise book or folder. You could keep these photos separately on a keyed sheet, but we think there's an advantage to attaching them to something that also has information to report in it; a photo on a book is ideal here.

In summary, always make sure you follow school policy. Remember who the reports are for: the student and their parents or guardians, not some notional government figure, inspectors or prospective employers (who are more interested in a concise curriculum vitae and a good reference, than a discursive document on how you and your student thought they'd achieved in French this year). Try to commit yourself to reporting, try to be meaningful and try to include real advice. If you do these things, then reporting becomes valuable for you, as well as for the student. Without these things, reporting becomes meaningless, onerous administration.

Some concluding remarks

Earlier in this chapter, we referred to 'gut instinct', and, indeed, this phrase is often used by teachers with reference to marking and assessment. New teachers are often worried that they don't have this attribute, that maybe they lack an essential gene for teaching! The reality, of course, is there's no such thing as literal gut instinct. What passes for this expression, is really a mixture of two things: observation and experience. You don't have to have a special facility to tell the difference between good work and bad: just look at it or read it. The more often you scrutinise work and apply formal criteria, the better you'll get at it. Eventually, you'll acquire the so-called gut instinct. The upshot of this is, you'll be slower to assess when you start teaching than you will be later on.

A word of advice: gut instinct can be dangerous. We know teachers who can run an eye over a piece of work and assess it in seconds, and they often prove to be right. This is, however, a dangerous game, and can lead to unfairness and mistakes. As suggested above, use gut instinct to rank-order a batch of work, but then, when you mark thoroughly, make sure you have your formal criteria close to hand, and read all the work. Marking, like reporting, has to be done with purpose and conviction.

Being fair to everybody

Putting work (note, not students) in rank order, is often necessary when you first start marking for assessment purposes, but when you've got used to it, often it's useful to mark in alphabetical order to facilitate the filling of mark-books. Make sure you don't always mark from A to Z; go the other way sometimes, so the people further up the alphabet don't always get you tired, fed up and with lots of other similar bits of work already in mind. Try not to have preconceptions about the work you're going to mark (this is very difficult). We always have to resist the temptation to mark all the good stuff first – apart from being unfair, it makes the tail-end of the marking depressing and you finish, feeling useless as a teacher. Never put the more illegible (and there will be students with awful hand-writing) work to the end. You'll be tired by then and likely to mark down through irritation. Unless presentation is an assessable issue, try not to confuse the look of the work with its content. Separate these aspects. If presentation is an issue for you, admit your prejudice to the student and suggest they word-process their work. Students with terrible presentation, are often incredibly proud of the improvement a well presented piece of word-processed work can make to assignments.

Praise and over-praise

We've repeatedly emphasised how important it is to always find something to praise in a student's work. This is sound advice, but make sure that you're finding something genuine to praise. Don't be overly effusive, and don't over-praise minor things. Most students have an accurate notion of their strengths and weaknesses, and to over-praise a piece of work that isn't very good (relative to their own capabilities), is patronising and destroys your credibility in their eyes. Moreover, undeserved praise can give some students an inaccurate reading of their actual progress, with potentially disastrous outcomes in public examinations.

It's even worse though to short-change on praise than to be too generous. There are few things that rankle with students so much as teachers who don't find good things to say about their students' best efforts. Here are some spoken and written expressions that we like to use when students deserve hardy acclamations.

Spoken

- 'You're really sharp. That was a great answer.'
- 'Thanks for showing me how to use that computer. You're a brilliant teacher!'
- 'What a star you are! You haven't given up, and now you've solved the problem.'

Written

- These scores just keep getting better and better. That's what happens with maximum effort.
- This reads like a best-selling novel. I'm really looking forward to your next piece.
- Your work is a joy to read.

Always remember that all students can and do make significant progress in terms of their own capabilities. While the rate and steps of progress vary quite considerably between different students, they often represent impressive headway for individuals. In this respect, it makes more sense to get students to improve their performance against their previous best rather than against the achievements of their peers. Doing better today at what the same student did yesterday, is always worthy of the highest praise.

What your mentor should do for you

Your professional effectiveness and your reputation will rest heavily on the published examination results of the students you teach. That doesn't mean that all these students have to achieve straight As; but you will be expected to have accurately calibrated their prior learning level and to have helped them to improve against their previous best. So sharpen those assessment and recording skills in order to gauge your value addedness – that is, what you, as a teacher, have added to a student's measured learning outcomes. With this end in mind, here's what your mentor should arrange for you, in terms of observation and practice.

OBSERVATION

These are some of the more important observations you need to make.

- Sitting in on departmental moderation meetings. These are designed to reach agreed upon, 'objective' grades (typically A–G) and levels (National Curriculum 1–10), to be awarded to students at critical moments in their school careers (for example, at the end of Key Stage 3 Statements of Attainment). Teachers normally submit samples of work that they judge to represent top, middle and bottom range performances, and other teachers check the work to see if they agree. Eventually, through a process of agreement, disagreement, arbitration and plea-bargaining, a final grade or level is recorded. Watching this process, won't only help you to make accurate assessments against standards expected of students of particular ages, it will also provide you with valuable insights into inter-departmental co-operation and negotiation.

- Shadowing teachers who are marking assignments, examinations, projects and tests. Initially, it's helpful to look at a sample of teacher-assessed work, representing a fairly wide range of grades or levels, so that you'll start to get a feel of how performance is measured against attainment criteria. Ask the teacher for explanations of the grades or levels she or he awards.

- Attending inter-departmental meetings where whole-school marking policies are discussed and developed, for example, standard correction codes for spelling mistakes across the curriculum. Such meetings often involve fairly senior staff – heads of department, deputy headteachers and the like – so you will gain valuable insights into the etiquette and practices of professional communication and consultative decision-making.

- Watching lessons where assessments are made on the basis of 'live' performances: gymnastics awards and sports trials, performing arts auditions, practical music tests; oral tasks in English and modern languages. In those examples, assessments are often based on formally defined criteria, but look out also for the large amounts of informal 'pat-on-the-shoulder' assessments that go on in classrooms, laboratories, workshops and sports fields whenever students and teachers interact: 'What an excellent Spanish accent you've got'; 'Top marks for using the correct safety procedures when you heated that chemical'; 'What a beautifully designed shopping trolley you're making'; 'That jump is getting two centimetres higher every week'.

- Seeing how teachers provide achievable yet challenging tasks for their students, based on what the teachers have assessed the students are capable of doing. For example, if a student is writing coherent sentences, the next step might be to provide learning opportunities that will help her or him to arrange sentences into paragraphs.

- Looking at sessions when teachers explain to students how their work will be assessed: 'You can only get 50 per cent of the marks on this paper for factual recall; the other 50 per cent is earned by weighing up the evidence'. This kind of information needs to be made explicit to students if they're to know how important it is, in some assignments, examinations and tests, not to submit 'write all I know, content-laden work'. It's also important for you to see the different ways in which teachers mark their students' work against clearly defined criteria which is understood by both parties. In A Level work, some teachers in our school, including us, explain to students that their grades will be enhanced two points upwards during their first term, and one point upwards during the second term. This gives them time to settle into the new courses and to gain confidence before their work is assessed on strict examination board criteria from the third term onwards.

Don't forget, on the reporting front, to look at some actual school reports. They're usually more detailed than the cursory, 'Satisfactory but could do better', comments that teachers dished out in earlier decades. Typically, they'll include an attainment letter Grade(A–E) and an effort number score (1–5). Rather confusingly, A usually denotes maximum attainment, and 5, maximum effort. These grades and scores will normally be supplemented with one or two paragraphs of constructive comments.

PRACTICE
- Having observed teachers carrying out assessments and having picked up a rough approximation of how different performances are recorded as grades or levels, get stuck in yourself. Ask your mentor to let you mark a set of assignments and tests that have been previously marked by experienced teachers (with the marks recorded on a separate sheet), which are fairly representative of a given attainment range. Then compare notes and mark some more samples, calibrating upwards or downwards or – if you've hit the right level straightaway – maintaining your marking pitch, in line with the teacher-assessed work.
- Acquire lots of practice in setting realistically challenging work for your students, based on your assessment of what they're capable of doing. Prior observation will help you here, but actual practice is your best ally. Don't get disconcerted if this skill takes quite a bit of time to accomplish. It's something that even the most experienced of teachers have to work hard at.

135

• Strive to adopt the same procedures for reporting to students on their progress and of explaining to them how the quality of their work will be judged, as those used by their regular teachers. Again, lots of observation of good practice will assist you in these tasks. So don't jump into the deep end too quickly. If you do, you'll make mistakes, and your students will give you lots of stick – whether you under mark or over mark their work.

Action points

1 Make sure you don't become bogged down in a legalistic interpretation of a whole Statement of Attainment – if you think the student has demonstrated even one aspect of a Statement of Attainment, give her or him credit for it. We're looking to reward achievement, not deny it.

2 Before assessing, arrange the students' work into rank order, using gut instinct, and assess the top and bottom candidates as firmly as possible. This will help you assess the others.

3 Make sure you assess the standard of students' current work against what they need to achieve, not against some notional standard of what they should have achieved by that age.

4 Make your recording for individual students as simple and accessible as possible. If you can do it in a few pages in a mark-book, all the better.

5 Make your recording an integral part of your work.

6 Any assessment that you make, should be explained to the student and used to generate advice for future performance.

7 Ensure that you follow up on advice. If it isn't checked, it may not be done.

8 Set single rather than multiple targets – you must make the students believe they can realistically achieve the work you give them.

9 Follow your school's policy on reporting, but remember who the reports are really for: the students and their parents or guardians.

10 Commit yourself to reporting and marking; otherwise, these tasks become an onerous nuisance. They're an important part of your relationship with your students.

11 Avoid pre-judging work to be marked.

12 Don't penalise content because of presentation.

13 Don't over-praise. Always praise, but do so realistically.

14 Aim for individual assessment, whenever possible, against previous best, rather than against peers.

CHAPTER 6

Professional development

The process of becoming an effective teacher is something that will continue throughout your professional life. In recognition of this fact, the DfE regard Initial Teacher Training as the first stage in a teacher's long-term career development. DfE criterion 2.6, Further Professional Development, requires that newly qualified teachers should have acquired, in initial training, the necessary foundation to develop:

2.6.1 an understanding of the school as an institution and its place within the community
2.6.2 a working knowledge of their pastoral, contractual, legal and administrative responsibilities as teachers
2.6.3 an ability to develop effective working relationships with professional colleagues and parents, and to develop their communication skills
2.6.4 an awareness of individual differences, including social, psychological, developmental and cultural dimensions

2.6.5 the ability to recognise diversity of talent including that of gifted pupils

2.6.6 the ability to identify special educational needs or learning difficulties

2.6.7 a self-critical approach to diagnosing and evaluating pupils' learning, including a recognition of the effects on that learning of teachers' expectations

2.6.8 a readiness to promote the moral and spiritual well-being of pupils.

That is quite a tall order, but it can be more concisely defined as: an understanding of school and community cultures; a knowledge of the pastoral, contractual, legal and administrative duties of teachers; an ability to develop good communication skills and an effective rapport with colleagues and parents; an awareness of the influence of psychological and sociological factors on the individual and cultural development of students; a capacity to recognise diversity of talent, and to evaluate and diagnose learning needs; a self-critical awareness of how teacher expectations affect student learning; and a willingness to foster the moral and spiritual well-being of students.

We'll start with the school and the community.

School and community cultures

Individual schools and individual communities have cultural lives of their own, each deserving their own distinct analyses. So don't be too rigid in your thinking. What goes down well in one school (for example, students addressing teachers on first name terms), might be proscribed in another school. Similarly, different communities generate different expectations of their feeder schools. For instance, parents in blue-collar, urban neighbourhoods, might expect the schools that their children attend to be tough on discipline. By contrast, parents from tree-lined, middle-class suburbs are perhaps more likely to support an informal, progressive school ethos. These observations are, to be sure, generalisations, so you'll have to judge the cultural climate of the school and community in which you work on their own terms. It should also be borne in mind that the schools serving a particular community often have their own unique, cultural styles, some of which reflect prevalent communal values, others which offer a different vision.

We're going to make the above points more vivid by focusing on the school and community where we work as teachers.

The school is purpose-built and is situated on the outskirts of a large northern city. It's a comprehensive school and it was opened in 1967. The suburb which it occupies is predominantly urban, white, working class, and has about 30,000 residents. The school admits students from the immediate community and from wide surrounding (including rural) areas. There are currently some 1800 students on roll.

The community's coal-mining past is celebrated by a large, textile-woven picture in the school's main foyer, which displays the area's coal-rich underbelly. A nearby pub, The Miners' Arms, also declares the neighbourhood's colliery heritage.

Today's residents are substantially of new working-class stock, more likely to be employed in service occupations than in hard hat, heavy industries. There's still a blue-collar feel about the place though, mirrored, in part, by the local Working Men's Club and the fish and chip shops which serve dinner, tea and supper, in that order.

Some managerial and professional families have moved into the area. They're more likely, however, to live on private estates and in semi-detached houses than on the council estates and two-up two-down terraces of their less well-paid and sometime unemployed neighbours.

It's from these various sections of the community that the school draws its students. The school seeks to build strong relationships with parents and other members of the community through a Parent-Teacher Association (PTA), and by participating in local events, like the town brass band. While it is difficult to gauge precisely what the parents of our students expect from us teachers, we sense that many of them want the school to provide:

- high standards of behaviour and dress
- firm but fair discipline
- good results in public examinations
- access to higher education
- little or no truancy
- regular homework
- success in sporting events.

The school scores highly on all counts: students wear a uniform (sixth formers wear office style attire); most students are very well-behaved; discipline is fairly tough, but seems seldom resented; league tables of public examination results are above the national average; about 60 per cent of students continue into the Sixth Form and some 75 per cent of A Level students move on to higher education; attendance averages around 95 per cent; homework is regularly set, marked and monitored; and there is representation at city, county and national level in sports.

Against the criteria that it believes the local community wants and which constitute its stated agenda, the school is meeting its aims through rather formal, traditional practices. But how does its ethos and mode of operation fit with your priorities? Would you like to work in our school? If your answers are in the affirmative, you'll settle in well. If, however, you prefer a more easy-going, progressive environment, you'll probably encounter some difficulties. This theme has already been touched upon in Chapters 1 and 4, but we want to consolidate and add to what has already been said.

Here is what we advise.

- Whenever possible, find out as much as you can about the school in which you might want to work long before accepting a post. You can begin by asking the school to send you its prospectus, along with the application form. The prospectus will probably give you a good idea of what the institution stands for. If you decide to submit an application, inform the school that you would be happy to attend a pre-interview visit for an informal talk and a look around. Useful people to talk to on such visits, are school caretakers (they can brief you on most things you'll need to know), school students, and class teachers (namely, the ones who teach rather than manage!).

   If the school doesn't arrange pre-interview visits but, nevertheless, offers you an interview, arrive early and take a walk around the neighbourhood, observing its ambience and character. Prior to the interview, you will normally have the chance to chat to staff and students. Don't underestimate the importance of these informal talks: you are being sized up and you have a chance to size up the atmosphere during them. If you don't like what you hear and see, withdraw your application before the interview. If things seem right, go for it.

- Assuming you've done well at the interview, and have been offered and accepted a post, arrange to visit the school and your department before you start the job. Ask your head of department to let

140

you spend some time during the visit shadowing an experienced member of staff. It's useful to extend the shadowing to pastoral (for example, form registration time) as well as curriculum (principally, class-teaching time) sessions. That way, you'll get a broader impression of the school's ethos, expectations and practices. This will help you to get tuned into the cues and signals that the particular regime gives out. I remember working in an inner-city primary school where the wearing by teachers of suits and formal dress intimated that the wearers probably had job interviews later in the day! By contrast, when teachers come to work in jeans at the comprehensive school where I'm currently employed, you can be pretty sure they're taking students on a field trip or attending the Year 11 leaving party.

Dress codes aside, use the visit to become acquainted with other important conventions and procedures: are students and staff on first name terms, are students expected to stand up when a teacher enters a classroom, who is the first port of call when a student walks out of a lesson without apparent good reason, does the school proscribe whole-class detentions? The more conversant you are with the way things are done, the more you will act like an professional when you get on the pay roll.

- When you start your first or new teaching job, you'll need to figure out how you, the institution and the community are going to work together. If all three are already on the same wavelength, that should be easy. But what happens if you find yourself in a school and a neighbourhood whose culture is at odds with your own beliefs and values? There are a number of options here: start looking for another post or succumb to the institutional and community culture, are the two extremes. At some point on the continuum, however, you might choose to strike a balance between what you can realistically hope to achieve and what senior staff and local parents are prepared to allow. This is roughly the position that we, the writers, occupy in our present posts.

Our school is rather formal, and so too, we sense, are the expectations of our students' parents. We, by contrast, have rather unceremonious leanings. That said, we wear suits and ties, are addressed by students as 'Sir', and sometimes assume the role of 'Mr Don't Mess With Me' when doing a tough substitution. By way of equanimity, we loyally protect our form members from the cruel and unusual punishments that certain colleagues might want to give them, we dance in a preposterously silly manner at our students' end of school leaving events, and we treat most of the students, most of the time, with the courtesy, respect and understanding they deserve.

In short, we don't put blind allegiance to some wholesale institutional culture before our own principles and professional judgements. Nor, in our view, should any teacher. We're not suggesting, however, that you become 'counter-culture warriors', if what you believe in, doesn't square with some of the things that the school values. There are entirely legitimate ways in which your reasonable aspirations can influence and, sometimes, change institutional practices.

To cite actual examples, two staff forums in our school (one involving a secret ballot), significantly influenced whole-school policies on the distribution of teachers' salary enhancements and on the issue of whether the institution might seek to opt out of City Council control. The upshot of these democratic gatherings, was that more staff received pay rises (excellent!), and the school made it clear that it wanted to stay with the City Council – which, thankfully, in our opinion, it has.

In our dealings with the community, parents are usually the most important bearers of the local norms and values that affect our work. In keeping with the school's rather formal character, we usually call parents, Ms, Mrs or Mr, but introduce ourselves as, Tim Crawley and Paul Stephens. We make appointments to see them at Parents' Evenings, but invite them to come by whenever they want to have a chat (more about parents in the section called *Colleagues and parents*).

Parents apart, we're not directly involved with other members of the community. That doesn't mean that you won't be. If, for example, you become a careers teacher or get involved with vocational courses, you'll almost certainly liaise with local private and public employers. Supposing, for example, you teach on a GNVQ Advanced course in Business and Finance, Science, or Tourism and Leisure, you'll need to play an active role in negotiating and procuring appropriate work placements for your students during the vocational parts of their programmes. It's very important though to realise that school and work cultures don't always go hand in hand. It would be insensitive, for instance, to promote green values in personal and social education lessons, while simultaneously placing GNVQ Advanced Science students in a local factory which short-changes on employee Health and

Safety measures, produces chemical weapon systems and pollutes the local environment.

Extreme you might think, but we've got an armaments factory up the road from our school! So, if you have dealings with neighbourhood employers, impress upon them that the school will only arrange placements in organisations that treat their employees with proper care, that produce ethical products and services, and that adopt environmentally-friendly practices.

Now it's time to turn to the pastoral, administrative, contractual and legal responsibilities of teachers.

Pastoralia, administration, contracts and the law

It sounds like an exotic blend of coffee, but pastoralia actually refers to the overseeing, protecting and supervising of the students in the teacher's charge. Administration has to do with paper work – too much of it (but, post the December 1993 Dearing Report, things are improving). The DfE reference to contractual and legal responsibilities covers a wide field, but we'll focus on two of the most important issues: under contracts, pay and conditions of employment; under law, health and safety.

We'll begin with pastoral responsibilities.

Caring for your students

Some people think caring about students is akin to what goes on in prisons: roll call, banging up, exercise in the yard, grub up, and – in between times – a bit of instruction and some moral training. At the other extreme, are those who adopt a 'students know best, so let them do what they want' approach: anything goes with this view. Most teachers are somewhere in between these two extremes. We err towards the progressive part of the continuum, but the institutional culture of our school is rather formal. So how do we deal with this potential tension?

- We believe that pastoral care should be premised on looking after our students, not policing them. We do our best to create a warm non-coercive, relaxed, environment, where respect for each other and reasonable behaviour, give or take the odd lapse, is seen as natural rather than enforced.

143

- We assiduously avoid terror-tactics at all times. Some self-styled pastoral managers pride themselves on frightening students into early submission when they enter secondary school in Year 7. A particularly horrifying example of this occurred in a school, where I worked, when a deputy headteacher plucked out alleged miscreants from their classes during an assembly, humiliated them in public, and stomped around, thumping furniture. Such behaviour, in our view, is unprofessional, unethical and very ineffectual in the long run.
- We place more emphasis on good intentions than on outward but resented adherence to rules. Students in our classes know we're much more concerned about whether they'll share their sandwiches with a friend who has forgotten hers than if they're wearing the right shade of regulation blue sweater.
- We always show sympathy and give emotional support to students who are experiencing difficulties, whether at school, home or elsewhere. We have broad shoulders and our students know this. Never make a student feel that she or he is intruding on your time if they want to talk about a problem. Always be approachable: students value that quality.
- In our roles, as form tutors, we're as protective as we reasonably can be towards those of our students who are being chased by other teachers: 'I know Dr Hemingway is understandably irritated with you for not handing in your homework. But I've told him you're a good student and persuaded him not to give you a detention. Make sure though that you get the homework to him by tomorrow – deal?' Apart from it being right to support your students, there is a payback: students have huge respect for teachers who stand up for them. Moreover, they're unlikely to misbehave in your presence.
- We don't regard our pastoral responsibilities as somehow separate from our curriculum duties. In our classrooms, students know they're free to talk to us frankly and openly without embarrassment or fear of punishment. They can praise or criticise us, provided this is done constructively and courteously. As I said in Chapter 4, my students recently told me that I talk too much in lessons. I've acted on this observation, by introducing more group work, an initiative that has been well received by the students.

The strategies we have outlined above, usually generate favourable behavioural and learning outcomes. These outcomes don't threaten the pastoral objectives of the school because our students are generally well behaved and hard working. At the same time, we, as teachers, are largely able to achieve these objectives without compromising our belief in the view that pastoralia should be about establishing an atmosphere of warmth and concern rather than creating a climate of fear.

We think it helpful to conclude this section on student care with some important observations and words of advice on child abuse. This disturbing and harrowing behaviour can be examined under the four broad categories listed below.

1 Physical abuse – any non-accidental injury to a child, or where injury was knowingly not prevented. Examples include: hitting, the administration of poisonous substances and not preventing a child from engaging in unreasonably dangerous activities.
2 Sexual abuse – involving a child in any sexual activity that may or may not include physical contact. Examples include: touching genitalia and involvement with pornography.
3 Emotional abuse – psychological ill-treatment or rejection of a child. Examples include: threats, unreasonable expectations and consistent lack of love and affection.
4 Neglect – failure to meet the basic and essential needs of a child. Examples include: leaving a child alone and unsupervised, and not seeking medical attention when a child obviously needs it.

If you notice emotional or physical symptoms that give rise to suspicion (for example, constant self-deprecation or frequent bruising), discuss your concerns with the headteacher and with a senior member of the pastoral staff (for example, a deputy headteacher or a year head). A decision will then be taken as to how the situation will be investigated and who will be involved in this process.

If a child tells you that she or he has been abused, or if you have strong suspicions that abuse has occurred, follow the same procedures. It's also helpful to record, in as much detail as you can remember, what the child has told you in her or his words, and, where appropriate, to make a note of any suspicious signs. This information can then be passed on to appropriate colleagues.

It's vital that confidentiality in matters of suspected child abuse be considered at all times. This will minimise the risk of stigmatisation of the child and family. That's why it's important to go through the right channels. Ensure too that child protection monitoring records are kept centrally with the headteacher. Access to such records within the school should be restricted to designated staff, and recorded when consulted.

Our school's Pastoral Managers, in liaison with local Child Protection and Education Welfare Officers, are currently seeking to draw up a School Child Protection Policy. The intention is to implement agreed procedures, so that all staff will have access to an explicit code of practice in dealing with matters concerning the maltreatment of students. Find out if your school has such a policy, and, if it has, stick to it in any action you might decide to take. If a policy doesn't exist, confer with senior pastoral staff to find out what procedures to follow.

Good pastoral care, whether dealing with routine or more serious matters, is importantly linked to effective administrative skills. You've got to keep tabs on what's going on in your students' lives, to be able to deploy your efforts in a way that achieves maximum benefit. Are your students frequently absent; have they received their dental and medical checks; what do their own statements on Records of Achievement reveal about their personal growth and learning; have they been referred to the local Education Welfare Officer?

Administration
Being an effective administrator means being able to impose order on what might otherwise appear chaotic. Your main administrative duties as a teacher are likely to fall within these two headings: form matters and recording of students' progress. Given that Chapter 5 deals with the recording of students' progress, this section will only consider the first issue.

Form matters
In our school, out of some one hundred and five full-time teachers, eighty five have pastoral responsibilities for forms. Chances are that you will be a form teacher.

In the average secondary school, reckon on a form size of about 28 students in Years 7 to 11, and about 16 students in Years 12 to 13. Your first daily responsibility will be to take the register. Here are a few do's and don'ts about the register.

• Do record attendances and absences accurately and neatly, and keep your register up to date (including current addresses of students, and home and emergency contact telephone numbers). Remember the register is an official document which will be looked at by senior pastoral staff, and, possibly, by support professionals like educational welfare officers and educational psychologists. Even fire-fighters might need to consult your register in the event of an emergency exiting of the building, to check who was originally on the premises. Keeping a good register is an important measure of your professionalism.

- Do insist on absolute silence when you take a register; distractions lead to mistakes. Students are usually reasonable about this, especially when you tell them that they can talk when the register is done. Once you've taken the register, conduct a head count of students and nominate two students to do likewise. This simple procedure provides an effective check on the calling out of names.

- Don't enter a student as present in the register unless she or he is physically in the form room. Comments from students that Arif is here, but he's seeing Ms Doherty must not be relied upon for purposes of recording a presence. Visual confirmation by you is vital.

- Follow up all absences, and record the reasons for non-attendance in the register, using the coding system used by your school. For example, where we work, a red circle around a black S, denotes a student was absent owing to permitted study leave. The usual procedure for absences not involving school events, like a geography field trip, is for the parents to write you a brief explanatory letter, which you sign and date on receipt and file for possible future reference.

Other administrative tasks that you'll probably encounter as a form teacher include: writing references for school leavers (build up an inventory of suitable comments), dispatching and checking the return of numerous parental reply letters concerning on-site vaccinations, Parents' Evenings, etc. (keep lots of copies of form name lists), and weekly monitoring of students' work record books (incorporate important observations from parents, students and teachers into your own file, for future use in other documents, for example, end of year reports).

As far as storing paperwork in an easily retrievable way is concerned, here are a few practical hints.

- Have three sturdy wallet files entitled, 'Form', 'Subject' and 'Other', with you at all times: it's amazing how quickly these will fill up.
- Keep three document trays in your form room with the same headings. Empty those non-confidential contents of your wallet files that deal with pending issues into these trays. Once the items have been dealt with, promptly recycle any documentation that won't be needed in future.
- Ensure that confidential documents, for example, student reports, medical notes and address lists, are placed under lock and key.
- Use clearly signed notice boards in your form room for important public information: emergency exiting procedures, forthcoming social events, form duty rosters, etc. Leave a space for your students to put up their notices and posters.
- Whenever possible, keep non-confidential, frequently needed information (for example, a form name list) on a computer file, to facilitate quick and easy retrieval: both on-screen and hard copy.

The contract

When you're offered a teaching post, you'll receive a contract of employment. Without going into all the small print, this will provide information on: how your salary will be assessed (actual salary details will probably be posted to you at a later date); statutory pension arrangements; and duties expected of you.

Teachers taking up their first appointment will have their 'spine points' (nothing to do with osteopathy!) assessed, and will be paid a salary commensurate with the assessed spine point. There are currently eighteen spine points (0–17) for classroom teachers. As at 1 April 1994, spine point 0 is worth £11571, and spine point 17 provides £31323. Your position on the Pay Spine, will be determined by the governing body of the school where you're employed. The main criteria for this are: qualifications, experience, responsibilities attached to the post, recruitment and retention (shortage subject specialists might gain here), professional excellence, and Special Needs duties.

When you decide to resign, perhaps in order to gain promotion in another school, the usual minimum periods of notice are:

- two months prior to 30 April
- three months prior to 31 August
- two months prior to 31 December.

Your other terms and conditions of employment will be covered by national and local collective agreements, copies of which will normally be available at your school.

The law

Teachers are, to use a common law precept, 'in loco parentis' vis-a-vis their students. This means that they take responsibilities for the young people in their care 'in place of parents or legal guardians'. The origin of the in loco parentis principle, dates from an 1893 court case: Williams *v* Eady. In this matter, a boy had easy access to a school conservatory in which phosphorus was stored. The boy got hold of the stuff, and burnt himself while playing with it. Subsequently, a court of law held that the phosphorus was potentially hazardous, and that precautions should have been taken to prevent access to the chemical. In his deliberations, the judge had to consider the standard of care required of a teacher in such circumstances towards the students in her or his charge. The judge made this ruling: 'A schoolmaster was bound to take such care of his boys as a careful father would take of his boys and there could be no better definition of the duty of a schoolmaster' (cited by Neil Adams, 1991).

The sexist but contemporaneous remarks aside, this dictum has essentially endured ever since. As Neil Adams (1991) puts it: 'We might now say that the basic position is one where teachers are required to take such care of pupils as good responsible parents would do, particularly bearing in mind the professional training they have received.'

The most important legal responsibility facing you as a teacher, from a care point of view, is to attend to the Health and Safety of your students (and also, but not 'in loco parentis', that of your colleagues). That's what the rest of this section will focus on.

Since 1 April 1975, all employees, including teachers, have been protected by the *Health and Safety At Work Act*. Section 7 of the Act places duties on employees to exercise reasonable care in ensuring that they don't endanger themselves or anyone else who may be affected by their work. It's also very important that employees draw to the attention of employers any 'near miss' incidents. Waiting for an accident to happen, won't do!

The list that follows on the next page, though not exhaustive, will give you an idea of the kind of Health and Safety issues that relate to work in schools.

149

Cloakrooms and sanitary arrangements

Make sure students only drink water from drinking water fountains and drinking water taps. These fountains and taps should be clearly sign-posted. Roller towels are hazardous and unhygienic; don't use them. Ensure that cold and hot water taps are provided in toilets, and that the hot water is hot enough without scalding. Make certain that any projecting coat hooks don't cause a hazard.

Corridors, stairs, landings and floors

Find out if there's a school policy on moving about the building (for example, keeping to the left). Ensure that there are no combustible materials stored in stair wells, and that corridors are clear of unnecessary obstructions. See that the floors are resistant to slipping when wet or dry.

Doorways

Make sure that doorways are clear of obstructions, and that there are no dangerous protrusions on doors. Check that external access doors are unlocked when the buildings are occupied.

Fields, playgrounds and carparks

Are there any holes? Is fencing adequate and secure? I once worked in an inner-city primary school where holes in the fence appeared regularly, probably made by truanting students. Is all outdoor equipment properly maintained and inspected? Are car parking arrangements safe?

Fire-fighting

Note if fire extinguishers are available near exits, and ensure that this equipment is regularly checked. Be familiar with procedures for fire and other emergencies (practice drills and real events). Make sure that internal fire doors are not wedged back. Ensure that the fire alarm is audible and distinguishable from other sound systems (for example, the school bell).

First Aid

Make sure you know and comply with the school's procedures for dealing with incidents requiring First Aid and other medical treatment. Be sure to follow rules concerning medication. We refer any students who ask for medication to the school nurse.

Furniture

Never use furniture that's broken, has loose fittings and hazardous protrusions. Report all such instances to staff who have designated responsibilities for school fabric.

Heating and ventilation

Last winter, our school was closed to most of the students because the boilers couldn't cope with the freezing weather. The school heating and ventilation system should be able to heat a minimum of 10 cubic metres of fresh air per person per hour. The following temperatures, at a height of 0.5m above floor level, should be maintained during normal occupation when the external temperature is -1 $^{\circ}$C:

- 21 $^{\circ}$C in areas where occupants are lightly dressed and inactive (for example, medical rooms)
- 18 $^{\circ}$C in areas where the dress and activities of occupants are at an average level (for example, classrooms)
- 15 $^{\circ}$C in dormitories
- 14 $^{\circ}$C in areas where occupants are lightly dressed and engaged in vigorous activities (for example, sports halls).

As for heating and ventilation equipment, it should not emit hazardous fumes, nor should it be electrically unsafe.

Specialist areas

These include, for example, science laboratories, practical workshops and physical education facilities. Always adhere to the stipulated Health and Safety procedures for these areas. If in doubt, confer with the appropriate heads of department.

Whole-school and departmental policies

Know them and keep to them. Examples include: whole-school bans on correcting fluid and the obligatory use of protective clothing for craft, design and technology lessons.

There will probably be explicit guidelines in your school on Health and Safety reporting procedures. The important thing to remember, is to report actual and potential hazards right away, and to use the correct channels for doing this. Verbal communication (backed up, as appropriate, with a written report) to a Health and Safety Officer, a premises fabric officer or the headteacher are all acceptable.

On the subject of communication, the next section emphasises how important it is to be a good communicator in your relations with colleagues and parents.

Relations with colleagues and parents

Good schools are characterised by a sense of common purpose between colleagues, and also between colleagues and parents. When these parties work in harmony and co-operation, everybody – not least the students – benefits.

Colleagues

Most of your colleagues will be other teachers: 'equals' and 'superiors'. You might decide to make some of them your friends. It's also likely that you won't take to all of them. Whatever happens, always behave professionally in your working relations with colleagues: friends, or otherwise.

Here are some useful hints.

- Get acquainted quickly with routine protocol: is the headteacher addressed on first name terms by all staff; are all colleagues addressed formally in the presence of students; do some teachers have 'reserved' chairs in the staffroom? (Yes, they actually do!)
- Use appropriate communication channels when you want things done. I came unstuck recently, by failing to inform a deputy headteacher in charge of examinations, that I had booked the main school hall for a student debate. Had I spoken to him first, I would have found that the hall was being used for examinations at the time. The issue isn't just about logistical problems arising from failing to use proper channels; it also has to do with showing due professional courtesies.
- Never be offended if colleagues ask you to communicate with them in writing on professional matters. For example, a short note on how well a student in another teacher's form is doing in PE, is more likely to be filed and remembered than a passing remark. It is also a good idea to keep a copy of any significant written communications that you make with other colleagues. Bear in mind, however, that some

colleagues will take exception if you send copies of these communications to other staff before consulting the original recipients first.

- always be on good terms with these important people: caretakers, cleaners, office staff, school dinners staff and technicians. They do very valuable work (for far too little pay), and they deserve respect. Remember that when you need their help. Better still, remember it because these people are your colleagues.

Now it's time to consider parents.

Parents

Teachers have often been encouraged to keep a client-style distance with parents. The upshot is rather clinical sessions between teacher and parent during once or twice yearly meetings after school. These occasions are normally one-sided affairs, with the teacher praising or cajoling daughters and sons for managing or failing to measure up to the standards of the school.

We supplement formal appointments with 'pop in for a chat' sessions, preceded, where possible, by a phone call from parents to make sure we're around when they want to come. Effective teachers build good relations with parents by meeting them in a sociable, friendly setting. Home visits provide such settings (check first though that your headteacher approves), as do Parent-Teacher Association social functions. It's also a good idea to invite parents in to school to give 'expert' talks to your students: what teachers were like when they went to school; their recollections of 1950s television shows; what it's like to work in a coal-mine.

Remember that much of your communication with parents will be in written form; comments in their children's books and letters home will feature prominently. It's vital that all such written communications are courteous. Discourteous remarks, whether addressed to parents or their children, are provocative and unprofessional. But we sometimes learn from our mistakes, as I did a couple of years ago. I made the following comment in the work record book of a 14-year-old boy in my form: 'You'll regret it if I get any more complaints from other teachers'. Big mistake! His mother took understandable exception to this rather 'threatening' warning, and wrote a rejoinder: 'Dr Stephens, I wasn't happy with the nature of your recent comment in my son's work record book, and would like to discuss the matter with you at the forthcoming Parents' Evening'.

I called the parent and, in the telephone conversation that ensued, I intimated that she was over-reacting: another communication error on my part. She didn't agree, so I invited her to the school for further discussion. But I knew I was in the wrong. I had displayed anger in the way I had communicated my feelings to the student and to his mother. It was for me to own up to this. When we met, her son in attendance, I said that my written comment was a response to critical remarks that another teacher had made in the boy's work record book. At the same time, I acknowledged that my 'warning' might reasonably be construed as threatening, and said I regretted the way I had phrased it. Instant success! The mother was conciliatory; so was the son. The rift had healed.

Be on good terms with parents. Make them your allies and co-workers. When home and school work in harmony, students feel secure, and favourable learning outcomes issue.

The next section explores some of the ways in which teachers try to understand and measure learning outcomes.

The importance of the 'ologies'

The study of learning outcomes, especially with regard to intelligence and achievement, forms a crucial part of pre-service and in-service training. This is where a knowledge of the 'ologies', notably, psychology and sociology, is very helpful.

Intelligence

There's no 'cut and dry' definition of intelligence. But we know how irritating it can be to come across sections in books that deal with concepts without actually defining them. So we'll give you a definition. Intelligence is the potential to learn from experience. That said, many psychologists claim intelligence can only be defined in relation to the potential to carry out particular activities. For example, you might show great potential to handle a computer, but limited potential to paper a wall. However, different societies tend to believe that certain types of activity require more intelligence than others. In Britain, for example, academic and professional activities, such as those of an eye surgeon, are generally claimed to require more intelligence than practical and craft activities, like those of a lorry driver.

Generally held by whom, you might rightly ask. Our answer is, what counts as an intelligent activity, is largely defined by the educational establishment: Secretaries of State for Education, public school headmasters, Oxbridge dons, peers of the realm, and one or two brigadiers, for good measure. Some fifty years ago, the then educational establishment introduced the 11+, a general intelligence test, and used it as the main method for determining the learning potential of 11-year-old students, prior to secondary education. The students who got the highest scores – the most intelligent – went to grammar schools, and became eye surgeons. Those with lower scores usually went to secondary modern schools, and became lorry drivers.

A key mover behind the introduction of the 11+, was Cyril Burt, who said things that the educational establishment liked to hear. He believed the test would identify bright children, regardless of their social class. However, by the 1950s, research was beginning to show that up to a quarter of 11+ decisions were inaccurate. Moreover, after Burt's death in 1971, there were allegations that his data and findings had been invented. The British Psychological Society disowned him, and, despite recent efforts to restore his credibility, the debate on his work is, at best, open.

Intelligence tests (IQ tests, as they're known) are still used by today's educational establishment: pretty much the same composition as before, and by the DfE and the School Curriculum and Assessment Authority. The tests are designed to measure people's aptitude (potential for acquiring skills) as independently as possible from any prior learning about the tasks set. There are two IQ tests that you might come across, especially if you work in Special Education.

- The Stanford-Binet Scale. This dates from 1916, and is the prototype of nearly all subsequent IQ tests. The 1985 version of this test, is devised to minimise ethnic and sexual bias in its questions.
- The Wechsler Intelligence Scale for Children (revised). This originates from an adult IQ test developed in 1939. It's supposed to measure 'pure intelligence', regardless of learning and good or bad teaching.

While IQ tests are used to measure ability, achievement (or attainment) tests are used to measure learning.

Achievement
Unlike intelligence, which refers to measurable learning potential, achievement refers to measurable learning competence. Being able to

swim, to obtain a C in GCSE Mathematics or to reach Grade 5 on the clarinet are examples of achievement.

In British society, achievement is closely linked to:

- social class (middle and upper-class students tend to achieve more than working-class students)
- ethnicity (students of African-black and Chinese origin are most likely to enter higher education, with white students and students of Indian origin next, and students of Caribbean-black, Bangladeshi and Pakistani origin towards the lower end)
- sex (females slightly out-perform males in GCSEs and A Levels, but slip somewhat behind males in higher education).

Once these factors have been accounted for, there is still, however, an element of student achievement that is attributable to what goes on in schools. Recent school effectiveness research, conducted by Sally Thomas, Desmond L. Nuttall and Harvey Goldstein (1993), showed that, when the prior achievement, ethnicity, free school meals entitlement (an indicator of low social class) and sex of 11,334 students aged 15 and above, who were entered for examinations in 116 schools, were taken into consideration, the following facts remained.

On average:
- students in girls' schools performed significantly better than students in mixed schools, but students in boys' schools didn't notably outperform their peers in mixed schools.
- students in voluntary schools (excluding Church of England schools) significantly out-performed students in county schools
- higher percentages of student attendance on one selected day in the 1990–91 school year were systematically associated with higher performance
- higher percentages of Year 11 students going into the sixth form were systematically associated with higher performance.

What can we infer from this, so far as teacher effectiveness is concerned? Here are a few pointers.

- Give girls some 'time-out' from boys in mixed schools. This can be especially helpful in the context of all-girl, physics and technology classes, where boys tend to assert their supposed 'mastery' by commandeering experiments and grabbing equipment.

156

- Make lessons exciting and vibrant enough to encourage students not to truant. Boredom is a major cause of high truancy rates.
- Encourage all your students to stay on at school beyond Year 11, thereby reducing their prospects of low pay and unemployment.

Other strategies associated with teaching effectiveness have already been identified in Chapter 4: do refer to these.

Remember too that all students can and do make significant progress, in terms of their own talents. These talents come in many forms.

Diversity of talent

'What a great public speaking voice you have, Aisha!'
'I hear you're a star when it comes to synchronised swimming, Tanya.'
'Three straight As in a row in home economics, Andrew – that's outstanding.'
'So you're taking two modern languages at GCSE, Rhian – I'm very impressed.'

Teachers need to respond to the many-sidedness of talent. Playing to the strengths of your students by applauding their best efforts and achievements, is always a good starting point. At the same time, it's important not to let students feel it's enough to be good at just one thing. This can restrict their aspirations and, in some cases, leads to damaging, self-fulfilling stereotyping. For example, assuming that black students make natural athletes and reluctant academics, is doing a grave disservice to them. Why not strive to be a great runner and a brilliant chemist? Similarly, girls won't be helped to develop all-round talents if some teachers assume they're better at English than mathematics. Nor will working-class students be encouraged to consider university studies, if teachers tell them they're more suited to practical rather than academic courses. These assumptions can seriously hinder the learning of black and female and working-class students, especially if the students start to believe that they can only succeed in some areas of the curriculum.

For these reasons, we are wary of Sir Ron Dearing's (1993) three-track view of talent in post-16 education and training. Sir Ron envisages the development of three educational pathways for students aged 16 and above as follows:

1 craft or occupational – giving students skills and knowledge directly linked to a craft or occupation through National Vocational Qualifications (NVQs)
2 vocational – a (rather confusingly described) midway path between the academic and occupational, leading to General National Vocational Qualifications (GNVQs)
3 academic – leading to A and AS Levels.

In fairness though to Sir Ron, he warns against students becoming prematurely committed to a narrow track. Yet we believe that this can happen if teachers think of talent in terms of distinct pathways. We prefer to encourage students to develop their talents on a broad canvas. We admit, however, that until parity of esteem between different types of excellence is generally recognised in our education system, narrowly defined and potentially damaging distinctions will endure.

Whatever talents your students display, you'll need to be able to evaluate them. You'll also have to be adept at diagnosing students' strengths and weaknesses if you want to create achievable learning programmes for them.

Evaluation and diagnosis

These two processes go together, but they have some distinctive features, so we'll look at each in turn.

Evaluation

Evaluation is underpinned by assessment. First, teachers measure student performance (assessment); then they make educational decisions based on the measurement (evaluation). For example, a teacher finds an 11-year-old student has a reading age of 16, and encourages the student to read suitably challenging books.

Essentially, evaluation is about setting achievable but stretching learning tasks. Get it right, and your students will gain increased self-esteem, and they'll make progress. Get it wrong, and they'll lose heart, and stand still or even lose ground. Existing standard tests and teacher assessment (formal and informal) will help you to establish the right pitch. We suggest the following guidelines.

• Don't assume that prior learning indicators (for example, last year's test scores with a different teacher) are necessarily accurate predictors of future progress. In particular, avoid negative stereotyping of alleged 'under achievers'. In your class, expect all student to achieve and then let them know you believe in them.

- Order learning tasks hierarchically, so that students are able to make realistic progress. Thus, you could set some content recall tests (How many Irish people died during the 1840's famine?) prior to evaluative work. (Assess the view that these deaths were preventable.)
- Give your students continuous practice (so-called over-learning), so that they experience the joy of success and the confidence that accompanies it.

Closely linked to evaluation is the diagnosis of learning needs.

Diagnosing learning needs

Diagnostic testing can be defined as a fine-tuned form of assessment. It gets down to the discrete factors which affect learning that aren't always revealed in standard assessment tests. For example, general reading tests might yield an approximate reading age, but they won't necessarily pin-point, as diagnostic tests do, specific strengths and weaknesses in a student's reading skills.

Diagnostic testing should be followed with diagnostic teaching, namely, the construction of an educational programme that enhances strengths and remedies weaknesses in the learning process. This is what is meant by the diagnosis of effective learning needs.

Diagnostic tests are usually administered by Special Needs teachers. In practice, these teachers tend to work mainly with less able students, but they also provide extension projects for gifted students.

Less able students

A student is described as being less able if she or he:

- has significantly greater difficulty in learning than the majority of students of similar age
- is making significantly less progress in one or more areas of the curriculum than in other areas.

Such individuals form part of the estimated 20 per cent of students following the National Curriculum who, at some time in their school career, have special educational needs (Dearing, 1993). Of these students, two per cent have learning difficulties and disabilities that are confirmed by legally binding 'Statements' of Special Educational Needs. As for the remaining 18 per cent, their needs, though less severe, are ratified by the Code of Practice arising from the Education Act (1993).

Special Needs, whether 'statemented' or 'codified', can be associated with: learning difficulties, physical and sensory difficulties, speech and language difficulties, and emotional and behavioural difficulties. This section focuses on Special Needs associated with learning difficulties.

A distinction can be made between general and specific learning difficulties. The first category refers to problems in all or most learning, the second category to problems in one or a few areas of learning.

General learning difficulties

These vary through mild, moderate and severe. Students with mild learning difficulties form the largest proportion of those needing special educational provision within mainstream schools. Don't be complacent here. Mild problems, for example, a 12-year-old student who has a reading age of 10, can get worse if suitable back-up isn't provided. It's important, in all cases, to look beyond a mere lack of progress to establish whether factors such as physical or sensory difficulties have a bearing on the problem. Partial deafness, for example, might be impeding listening skills. When in doubt, have a word with appropriate staff (notably, the Head of Special Needs and the school nurse) about your concerns.

Students with mild learning difficulties can often be successfully helped to follow the mainstream curriculum. The majority, with appropriate support (for example, some extra one-to-one teaching), will be able to manage in ordinary classes. It's helpful though to provide these students with very clear explanations and well-defined tasks.

Students with moderate learning difficulties experience quite significantly greater obstacles than those with mild problems. These students might include, for example, 12-year olds who have a reading age of 8. Special educational provision for such students will usually involve finely graded study programmes in basic subjects, with plenty of opportunities for 'over-learning' and revision. Sometimes this can be provided in ordinary classes. Other options include withdrawal groups, special classes and special schools.

Students with severe learning difficulties are usually educated in special schools. They need a great deal of individual attention. Learning tasks need to be set in bite-size, step-by-step sequences, and much of these must be tailored to each student's individual capabilities. The development of communication and self-help skills often figures prominently in learning programmes for students with severe learning difficulties.

Specific learning difficulties

It's important to identify students who appear to be of general average ability, but who encounter marked learning difficulties in certain areas of the curriculum, for example, mathematics. Sometimes these difficulties are due to undetected sensory problems, to disrupted or unsatisfactory teaching, or to emotional traumas. There are also some students who experience major problems with reading and writing in whom these causal factors aren't present. Such students are sometimes referred to as dyslexic.

Don't make the mistake, though, of assuming that students with specific learning difficulties should necessarily follow a 'slow learner' curriculum. For example, a student who is very articulate in spoken language but who finds writing difficult, will rapidly become under stretched and frustrated in an across-the-board programme for low achievers in English. In this case, more effective outcomes are likely to result if the student stays in ordinary English classes, but receives targeted support in writing skills. Other appropriate measures for students, with this kind of difficulty, include the use of a portable tape recorder to assist in note taking and playing to the strength of the student's oral competence by using plenty of spoken language.

It's now time to consider students who have special needs that are different from those of less able students, those whom the DfE defines as gifted.

Gifted students

We prefer the term 'very able' to gifted. There is an assumption of the prior bestowal of talent that needs no effort behind the idea of gifted. Yet, as teachers, we believe that excellence needs working at. But how do we define 'very able'? A very able student has outstanding potential or ability in one or more areas to the extent that she or he needs more attention than the teacher usually provides. Here are some of the indicators that might be detected, to varying degrees, in students who

161

have extraordinary ability and potential. The students :

- find usual resources and tasks superficial, and get impatient with easy things
- display rapid command and recall of information
- are intensely curious and ask deeply searching questions
- see beyond conventional, predictable patterns
- even when seemingly daydreaming, know exactly what's going on, and respond quickly and accurately to sudden questions
- make quick connections between theoretical principles and real events
- don't accept 'teacher knows best' because 'teacher says so'
- expect corroborative evidence and logical explanations
- are often quick-witted and catch on to humorous nuances with ease
- sometimes ponder over detail and deeper meanings to the extent that they don't write enough when subjected to time constraints; one of my most brilliant A Level students sometimes wrote a half page essay (which contained doctoral level insights) instead of the expected two and a half pages in 45 minutes
- employ advanced use of language in spoken and written work
- are astonishingly sure-footed in computing (often well ahead of IT teachers in this area!), engineering, mathematical and general problem-solving exercises
- display extraordinary physical ability, typically playing at city or county level
- exhibit superlative skills in visual and performing arts.

Unless schools provide special classes for very able students, teachers have to meet their learning needs in normal mixed ability settings. Rather than providing custom-made tasks for these students, we usually set them similar work to other students, but support and extend their creative and evaluative skills by encouraging their intellectual argumentativeness: 'Yes, that's a really sharp rebuttal of the textbook account Sarah; let's have your interpretation.'

We also use very able students as peer tutors. This places them in the role of 'teacher' to other students. Recently, for example, I asked four very able students to provide tutorial support to a student who entered a course midway through the first year of a two-year programme. They agreed to use some of their non-contact time to help guide the new entrant through the catch-up stage of his learning. The student benefits from working with peers who have recently made the journey he is starting. They gain much by revisiting ground already covered, thereby consolidating and adding to their existing knowledge and understanding. The peer tutors also know I have great faith in their ability – why else would I ask them to play such an important role in helping a newcomer settle into the course? This positive expectation boosts their self-esteem and increases their motivation to become even better scholars.

The expectations that teachers have of all students, less able, able and very able, are crucially linked to learning outcomes. This theme is taken up in the next section.

Teachers' expectations and students' progress

Have high expectations of your students' capacity to learn, and make sure they know this. Students have a tendency to live up to positive expectations and to live down to negative expectations. This observation is amply supported by research (for example, Alex Thio, 1989), as well as by our own professional experience. Students respond well, in both behavioural and learning terms, to teachers who make them feel successful. By contrast, they're likely to play up and to give up when teachers put them down.

The main beneficiaries of the positive self-fulfilling prophecy effect are:

- middle and upper-class students
- male students, notably, with regard to their alleged prowess in mathematics, physics and technology
- students from ethnic groups whom some teachers tend to regard as highly motivated, particularly, those of African-black, Chinese, Indian and white origin.

The main casualties of the negative self-fulfilling prophecy effect are:

- working-class students (especially if they're expected to leave their own culture at the school gate)
- female students, notably, with regard to their purported ineptitude in mathematics, physics and technology

163

- certain ethnic minority students whom some teachers expect to under-achieve or to only excel in limited ways, particularly, those of Caribbean-black, Bangladeshi and Pakistani origin.

It would be inaccurate, however, to assume that learning outcomes always match teacher expectations. Some students, for example, successfully challenge and resist negative stereotypes. This might partly explain why female students currently out-perform (though marginally) male students in GCSEs and A Levels. That said, female students are more likely than male students to be discouraged from entering high level courses in mathematically-based subjects. Bearing in mind that these courses often provide access to prestigious degrees and good incomes, it's important, in your own professional practice, to encourage female students to take them.

Similarly, in your work with working-class, Caribbean-black, Bangladeshi and Pakistani students, be on your guard not to lower your expectations of what these students can achieve. Moreover, don't assume that they are more suited to certain courses than others. This assumption nearly always works against them. For example, the inference that students from inner-city council estates are generally better at PE than English, or that Caribbean-black students are often more likely to succeed in performing arts than in mathematics, can have damaging self-fulfilling outcomes. There's nothing wrong with PE or performing arts, but all students are entitled to the expectation that they have the potential to succeed in all areas of the curriculum.

Teacher expectations, however, don't just concern the acquisition by students of required knowledge and skills. Society wants more than this. It is teachers, perhaps as much as parents and the media, whose task it is to shape the 'values' of our young people. The Government recently made this point explicit, by requiring schools to enter in their prospectuses, a statement of their ethos or shared values.

Morals and spirituality

The principle that schools should be involved in the transmission of societal values, is enshrined in the *Education Reform Act* (1988). The Act requires schools to attend to the 'moral' and 'spiritual' well-being of school students. The reference to 'spiritual', strongly implies a religious dimension. In that context, the Act also says that Religious

Education syllabuses must: 'reflect the fact that the religious traditions in Great Britain are in the main Christian while taking account of the teaching and practices of the other principal religions represented in Great Britain.'

Given too that DfE Competence criterion 2.6.8, links together the promotion of the 'spiritual' and 'moral' well-being of school students, it seems plausible to suppose that this criterion has a firm anchorage within a predominantly Christian framework. So where does this leave you, the intending or practising teacher? The official DfE position is that: 'All maintained schools must provide religious education and daily collective worship for all registered students and promote their spiritual, moral and cultural development.' (Religious Education and Collective Worship, Circular number 1/94, 31 January 1994.) However, teachers are not obliged to teach Religious Education or lead or attend collective worship, except where the law states otherwise in relation to some teachers in voluntary (for example, Roman Catholic) and equivalent grant maintained schools. Moreover, school students are not required to participate in Religious Education or collective worship if their parents decide to withdraw them from these activities.

Whether you're an atheist, an agnostic or a believer, it's likely that you'll be expected not openly to oppose the Christian components of Religious Education and collective worship in schools where a Christian ethos predominates. This doesn't mean that other religious beliefs will be excluded from what goes on in schools. On the contrary, the School Curriculum and Assessment Authority launched two model Religious Education syllabuses in January 1994, which have achieved a considerable degree of consensus among members of different faiths. The syllabuses have broken new ground by producing, for the first time, something that approaches a 'national curriculum' of Religious Education.

Designed to take up 5 per cent of the curriculum time, the syllabuses have a 51 per cent Christian content – 75 per cent is possible at some Key Stages. Students must also study Buddhism, Hinduism, Islam, Judaism and Sikhism. Between the ages of 5 and 7, students are expected to understand the importance of Christmas and Easter, and to grasp the idea of God as a loving parent.

If they study Judaism, they're supposed to comprehend the significance of the Torah and Hanukkah. Students aged 7 to 11 should learn how, for example, Jesus helped people, and how God was manifested in the Old Testament. Students who choose the Hindu option, must study the historical origins of that religion, and why its practitioners are required to proclaim non-violence.

In the 11 to 14 year age range, students should be able to discern the different emphases of the Gospel writers, and to recognise the influence of Christian values on social issues. The Islamic option includes: studying the Koran, an awareness of the different acts of worship and a knowledge of the life of the Prophet, Muhammad.

Teachers of Religious Education and teachers who work in voluntary schools, are more likely to be involved in the spiritual aspects of student learning than teachers of secular subjects and teachers employed in non-denominational county schools. However, all teachers are engaged in moral education, whether or not the dissemination of moral values is couched in religious terms. In that sense, you'll be expected to promote and to demonstrate, in your own attitudes and behaviour, certain universal principles. It is difficult to be overly prescriptive here, but we suggest you should do the following.

- Encourage students to challenge prejudice and repudiate discriminatory practices. You can do this by, for example, reminding students that Dr Martin Luther King broke unjust laws and endured months in jail to highlight the limitations of certain customary efforts which conformed to the letter of the law.
- Foster co-operativeness in human relationships. This might be developed by involving students in collaborative learning tasks, like designing and producing a classroom display. Other avenues could include joint problem-solving activities, for example, a group design and technology project on how to improve access to classrooms for people in wheelchairs.
- Persuade students to look beyond the parochial boundaries of their immediate environs, and to recognise and celebrate their global humanity. One way to do this, is to show, by your own example, that you buy products that are fairly traded and environmentally friendly. We find that young people are very favourably disposed towards initiatives like this.

On the issue of 'spiritual' growth, we suggest that you should be mindful of the following points.

- There are many different ways in which people seek to express their spiritual nature, so avoid notions of cultural and religious ascendancy in your teaching.
- It is important to let students develop their own spiritual insights, so encourage them to think independently and to ask critical questions.
- In our multi-faith world, it is right to engender a better understanding of different religions, so give students opportunities to reflect on and respond to, with due sensitivity, the beliefs and values that underpin diverse religious practices.

Don't feel overwhelmed by the wide range of professional development competencies that the DfE expect newly qualified teachers to start getting acquainted with. They aren't looking for a 'done and dusted' portfolio of skills. What they want, are foundation competencies, upon which future development will flourish. Teaching is a life-long process of learning, but getting the basics right is very important.

What your mentor should do for you

Professional development implies that Initial Teacher Training is only the beginning of a life-long process of learning and growth. It's important though that you start your first job with a secure footing. The observation of good practice will help you here, as will getting in some good practice. This is what we think you should be asking your mentor to arrange on the basis of 'watch and have a go'.

OBSERVATION

- Opportunities to observe extra-curriculum events, especially those involving parents and the local community. Tell your mentor that you'd like: to attend a Parents' Evening (and, who knows?, pass on some helpful comments, if appropriate); to shadow teachers during school trips; and to accompany teachers who are involved in community liaison work (for example, a Year 7 Head of Year, addressing students from a primary feeder school).
- The shadowing of the Special Needs teachers as they go about their craft. These are some of the most dedicated and skilled teachers in the profession. Watch how they relate to their students, see how

they coax them into learning, and pay particular attention to the ways in which they monitor their students' behavioural, cognitive and physical growth.

- A pastoral attachment to a form. Your mentor should be able to fix this up without much trouble. Before joining the form for registrations and other form time activities, arrange a thorough briefing on the correct protocol from the form teacher. This would include: how to take a register, and how to relate to the students in what are often non-teaching situations.
- If you're not teaching RE, the monitoring of some RE lessons. Note the extent to which these lessons promote the moral and spiritual growth of students. Be prepared for some wide variations here, from direct evangelism to more historical/sociological approaches. Attend some school assemblies, especially those involving collective worship. It's up to you whether you want to join in or not.

PRACTICE

As far as activities are concerned the following experiences are essential.

- Ask your mentor to arrange an interview between you and these important people: the headteacher (take the opportunity here to ask her or him for some useful tips when you attend job interviews), the deputy headteachers responsible for curriculum and pastoral matters (these senior colleagues are usually well acquainted with legal and contractual matters, so ask away, especially with regard to health and safety issues and your future career development).
- Circulate in the staffroom and get your mentor to introduce you to teachers from a wide range of different departments, newly qualified, as well as more experienced staff. Be friendly but not pushy, curious but not snoopy. Above all, don't be too chatty (it doesn't go down well with the older hands), and never sit in 'reserved' chairs!
- Book some time working with Special Needs teachers, both in mainstream and support classes. This is an excellent way to hone your individualised and group teaching skills. It's also immensely satisfying to see students with learning difficulties, as well as high flyers (though most of these will be in mainstream classes), making progress and enjoying their learning.

Action points

1 Strike an achievable balance between your teaching style and the institutional culture of the school and the expectations of the community.

2 Cultivate a relaxed, non-coercive pastoral atmosphere rather than a policed environment, be approachable and sympathetic, and stand up for the students in your care.

3 Get quickly acquainted with Health and Safety regulations, and act on them. Be alert also to the signs of possible child abuse. Use well-defined channels when you have to, and keep all child protection documents under lock and key.

4 Keep meticulously accurate, presentable, up-to-date registers, always checking roll calls with eyeball corroboration.

5 Adopt a simple and accessible filing system, using document wallets and corresponding document trays, headed, 'Form', 'Subject', 'Other'.

6 Keep to professional protocol in dealings with colleagues and parents, but supplement formal communications with more friendly overtures.

7 Consider educational issues which have an important bearing on chalk-face practice, notably, the psychological and sociological dimensions of intelligence and achievement. However, don't assume that prior learning or other indicators, like social class, are 'destiny': effective teachers make a difference.

8 Recognise that talents come in many shapes and sizes, and encourage all students seriously to consider staying on at school beyond age 16 – the post-compulsory curriculum is much more varied and accessible these days.

9 Use appropriate diagnostic procedures in order to enhance students' strengths and remedy their weaknesses, and give students plenty of scope to 'over-learn' (that is, to consolidate existing skills).

10 Remember that all students, whatever their abilities, can and will make progress if you make their learning goals achievable but challenging.

11 Watch out for any physical and sensory problems that might underlie behavioural and learning difficulties, and report any suspicions or findings to the appropriate colleague(s). Be sure to make the distinction between general and specific learning needs, and adapt your teaching accordingly.

12 Have high behavioural and learning expectations for all your students, and make sure they know this.

13 Become familiar with the statutory regulations on the teaching of religious education and collective worship.

14 Be a principled teacher; that is the best moral education you can give your students.

CHAPTER 7

Looking ahead

Looking ahead for you, probably means securing a first, a sideways or a promoted teaching appointment. We'll deal with that kind of anticipatory planning under the section, *Getting appointed*. Subsequently, this concluding chapter will focus on three new developments in schools that are beginning to have important implications for the professional work of all teachers. These developments are: the Government's implementation of the Final Dearing Report (December 1993); the growth of electronic learning environments; and the impact of school effectiveness and school improvement research on good practice.

Getting appointed

Usually, your first overture to the school where you want to work will be the posting of a completed application form, supplemented with a supporting letter and a curriculum vitae. It is vital that you get this part of the procedure right. Here is some advice.

The application

- If possible, word-process or type the details on the application form; otherwise they should be impeccably handwritten using black ink. Never short-change on the required details: you could literally be short-changing yourself with regard to salary entitlement, especially if you don't give full information on study, work and qualifications.
- Send a supporting letter of application (definitely word-processed or

typed) of no more than two sides of A4. The first side should high-light your generic strengths, focusing especially on transferable skills: 'My IT expertise is well-suited to the administrative and learning environments of forward-looking schools'. The second side should target your particular strengths to the specific requirements of the job: 'My successful teaching placement in an inner-city sec-ondary school, has prepared me well for work in an urban school such as your own'.

- Attach a concise (about two sides of A4) curriculum vitae, divided into these sections: Personal Details; Education and Qualifications; Employment; and Other Information. If possible, ring bind this copy with a transparent front cover and a cardboard back cover (this looks very professional), and enclose an additional loose-leaf copy (for ease of photocopying by the short listing panel).

The interview

Congratulations! If you've got this far, your application was well received.

- Get full details from the school about the syllabus(es) the successful applicant will be required to teach, and make sure that you can con-fidently answer, 'Yes', to the question, 'Are you competent to teach this course?'
- Arrange for a 'dry run' interview with a university tutor or a school mentor. This can prove invaluable in terms of getting an indepen-dent assessment of your communication and presentational skills, and of identifying areas for improvement.
- Normal attire and 'conventional' hairstyles are strongly advised. Headteachers generally prefer a 'professional' look. We know a headteacher who told an applicant, 'I wouldn't have invited you to an interview if I knew you'd turn up without a jacket', and another who enquired of an applicant, 'If you're offered this post, will you get a haircut?'
- Be prepared for two interviews, normally, both on the same day: an informal opportunity to meet key staff and to talk to students (don't you believe it; this is really a 'sizing up interview'), followed by a formal interview with senior teachers – usually, a head of department, the headteacher, and one or two deputy headteachers (a school governor might also be present).

- In addition to questions about your ability to teach particular courses, get ready for questions like these: 'What are your strengths and weaknesses?'; 'Should teachers stick to facts or should they promote values?'; 'Where do you see yourself in five years from now?' ('Bognor', is not the right answer!); 'If you're offered this post, will you be able to give us your decision today?'; 'How would you deal with a 16-year-old-young man who throws his exercise book on the floor when you tell him to stop talking and to get on with his work?' (role-play might feature here; we know a deputy head-teacher who, feigning a rebellious student, throws a clipboard across the room during interviews); and don't be left with nothing to say when that time-honoured chestnut, 'Is there anything you'd like to ask us?', rounds off the proceedings.

The system for informing the successful applicant that she or he is to be offered the job is generally rather brutal: after the last applicant has been interviewed, all the applicants usually wait in the staffroom while the interview panel deliberates; if the panel decides to appoint, the chosen applicant is informed on the spot by a senior teacher, and the unsuccessful applicants are thanked for attending the interview. If you're not appointed, do ask the senior teacher for a de-briefing. This is an entirely acceptable request, and could provide useful guidance for future interviews.

Let's assume though that you've made it on this occasion. So what's going to face you, teacher of the 1990s and beyond?

The dust begins to settle

On 2 August 1993, the Government accepted an interim report by Sir Ron Dearing on the future development of the National Curriculum. Sir Ron was asked to conduct further policy-oriented research during the autumn and to present his findings in a Final Report by the end of the year, on these issues:

- the future shape of the curriculum for 14–16-year-old students
- the time-frame for slimming down the curriculum
- the grading of students' attainment.

The Final Report arrived – on schedule – in December, 1993, and its main recommendations were accepted in full by the Government. The dust is beginning to settle!

How will this affect you, the intending or practising teacher? The reforms will help to liberate you from the bureaucracy and over-prescription which have hitherto prevented teachers from making the most of the National Curriculum. In concrete terms (and we're obliged to reacquaint you with some of the points made earlier in the book), this means that the following modifications have been made.

- The mandatory curriculum for 5–14-year-old students (English, Mathematics, Science, and Technology – including IT, History, Geography, Music, Art, PE, and, from 11 onwards, a Modern Foreign Language) is significantly streamlined, especially outside the core subjects of English, Mathematics and Science. What must be taught in every subject will now be confined to a kernel of compulsory content, thereby giving teachers more discretion over what counts as relevant knowledge beyond the kernel.
- The mandatory curriculum for 14–16-year-old students is reduced to a minimum of: full GCSEs in English, Mathematics and Science; short courses in Technology and a Modern Foreign Language; PE; Religious Education, and Sex Education. This frees curriculum time for other academic and vocational options. With regard to the vocational options, these will be designed to accommodate progression to post-16 vocational courses. Bear that in mind, in case you want to get better acquainted with NVQs and GNVQs during pre-service or in-service training.
- The 10-level scale at Key Stages 1–3, is simplified, by greatly reducing the number of Statements of Attainment at each level, and by terminating the scale at the end of Key Stage 3. The A*–G grading scale for GCSEs will still operate.

On the matter of timing

- The revised curriculum will become effective at Key Stages 1–3 in September 1995, for the 1995–6 school year.
- Subject to further consultation, revised GCSE syllabuses in National Curriculum subjects are likely to come on stream from September 1996.

Moreover, once the reforms have been implemented, if the Government follows Sir Ron's advice (which it generally does), no further major changes to the curriculum will be made until the year 2000. At last, we can start to nail the jelly to the wall! Another thing we can be fairly certain of, is that the kind of educational environment in which you'll be working, will be quite considerably different from the one you experienced when you went to school.

Electronic classrooms

In the fortieth anniversary edition of the *Beano* comic of 19 February 1994, the Bash Street Kids enter a new era: they get a robot teacher. Such is the pace at which IT in schools has developed, that we might be closer than we think to this form of automation. Tokyo University's Department of Architecture has already built a house that does everything from opening its own windows to looking for lost cuff-links. What's to stop schools from making similar headway by developing 'intelligent building' designs?

Imagine a classroom with a simple wall socket that connects students and teachers to an information superhighway of on-line reference libraries, and which hooks up schools to academic specialists via electronic mail. This vision of the future is rapidly becoming a reality: the US Federal Government is already legislating the required action, and BT is poised to send a learning environment down our own UK digital highway.

So much in the day-to-day running of the modern school looks for a computer solution – staff and student data handling, registration, reporting, and much more besides. We therefore emphasise what we've said throughout the book: invest as much time as possible during your Initial Teacher Training in getting to grips with IT. Your future success as an effective teacher will depend on this investment.

The computer is now poised to take over many aspects of lecture-style teaching. Picture a traditional Key Stage 3, whole-class mathematics lesson. When 30 students are grouped together because of similar age or similar ability, don't expect a uniform learning outcome when the teacher gives a lecture. Some students will struggle and switch off; others will be held back and become rapidly frustrated. One effective solution is to match learning tasks to the strengths and weaknesses of each student, by using individualised computer-based work schemes.

The software is already available to achieve that goal through a programme of tuition and problem-solving exercises which reinforce what has already been accomplished, coax students into stretching activities, monitor progress and provide feedback. For example, a US computer programme, *Success Maker* (from the Computer Curriculum Corporation), takes students through 16 strands of mathematics, including applications, basic operations and geometry. Students enter the programme at a level set by the teacher, and a diagnosis of what they achieve is stored by the software memory, so that future exercises are cognitively matched to the students' individual abilities. These exercises promote 'over-learning' (an essential feature of effective teaching), by revisiting already accomplished tasks, as well as providing extension work in new areas.

There are many more ways in which traditional teaching methods and conventional learning environments are being transformed in the electronic classroom. Who needs to learn long-hand arithmetic in the age of digital computers, when even mathematics professors use computers to prove their theorems? Why shouldn't a student with cerebral palsy, gain hours of learning time by using a predictive word processor that, as she or he keys a word, makes an intelligent guess at what the next word will be? What about using a CD-Rom (the computer equivalent of an ordinary CD) to bring the actual voice of President Nelson Mandela into a classroom discussion of civil rights?

The compelling logic behind these technological breakthroughs is that teachers need to get better at supporting student-centred learning. We still believe there is a place for the stirring rhetoric of a short, punchy lecture, but we advise you to put lots of effort into that other aspect of the DfE Subject Application Competency: the ability to plan and provide for individualised learning. We especially commend to you the deployment of IT, an important aspect of the DfE Class-Management Competency, in tailoring learning tasks to individual aptitudes.

It's now time to consider a final issue, the impact of school effectiveness and school improvement research on good practice.

School effectiveness and school improvement research

Schools can and do make a difference to what students achieve and how they behave. School effectiveness research seeks to find what characterises good practice (high expectations, fair 'discipline', and such like), while school improvement research tries to apply that knowledge in ways that make schools better.

This book has already distilled many of the recommendations of this research, but we have also cautioned against overly mechanistic approaches. What works well in one school, for example, students relating to teachers in an informal manner, might prove disastrous in a school where more conservative conventions are expected. Yet out of these differences, we might still be able to draw some generic features of effective teaching: the adoption, for example of a coherent whole-school policy that all students, teachers and parents know and respect.

We'll end this chapter by stating what research and our own professional work demonstrate are important elements of generically effective practice. Much of this is to reiterate, by way of summary and reinforcement, themes which have been developed throughout the book:

- lots of praise for genuine effort and achievement, and for responsible behaviour, coupled with unobtrusive, non-coercive discipline, and swift, consistent action to deal with outright laziness and disruptive behaviour
- the avoidance of brutalising, humiliating punishments, whatever the gravity of the alleged offence
- responsiveness to students' concerns and needs, and a willingness to help students with their problems
- the provision of opportunities for students to take responsibility for, and participate in, the running of their school lives (for example, student-centred learning tasks)
- good models of appropriate behaviour by teachers (for example, starting lessons on time)
- the keeping of the attention, interest and engagement of the whole class by making learning fun
- the ensuring that all students understand how to perform the tasks teachers set them or they set themselves
- the provision of intellectually challenging tasks (for example, questions that encourage students to become problem-solvers)
- the creation of a reasonably structured, focused learning environment which, at the same time, permits some scope for discovery-based inquiry
- the provision of a work-focused atmosphere, characterised by a high degree of on-task learning, and a minimum of distraction

- the creation of a limited focus within each lesson confined to specific points, and a fairly brisk (though not if students feel rushed), small-steps progression through learning tasks
- the maintenance of maximum communication between the teacher and all the students (for example, ensuring that all students are normally spoken to at least once by the teacher during lessons)
- the prompt marking and returning of all work, accurate but not unduly discouraging assessment, and the meticulous recording of students' progress.
- the encouragement of parental involvement (for example, helping with, but not doing, homework)
- staff commitment to an explicit and shared mission, which focuses on high behavioural and learning expectations, and the challenging of all negative 'isms' (notably, classism, disablism, racism and sexism).

In writing this book, we have had to evaluate our own practice. That has made us better practitioners because we have discarded from our teaching the things that don't work, and retained and strengthened the best methods. Throughout, the litmus test of what we believe constitutes effective teaching, has been the behavioural and learning outcomes of our students. Despite coming from neighbourhoods where low incomes and unemployment place great strains on many families, our students are well-behaved, and they achieve educational results that are above the national average. Above all, they're a joy to work with.

Good practice is more dependent on applying what is demonstrably effective than relying on vaguely felt hunches. We hope that the insights of our craft-professional knowledge and experience, the feedback from our students and the findings of the research reported in the book, will help you become an effective or a more effective teacher. One final thought: if your teaching replaces racism, sexism and other prejudiced viewpoints with an enlightened outlook, hearsay judgements with critical awareness, half-truths with honest scholarship, you will be doing your job well.

BIBLIOGRAPHY

Adams, Neil (1991) *Know your Rights: Teachers*. Plymouth: How to Books Ltd.

Badger, Bill (1992) 'Changing a Disruptive School'. In Reynolds, David and Cuttance, Peter (eds.) *School Effectiveness*. London: Cassell.

Brown, Sally and McIntyre, Donald (1993) *Making Sense of Teaching*. Buckingham: Open University Press.

Council for the Accreditation of Teacher Education (1992) *The Accreditation of Initial Teacher Training under Circulars 9/92 (Department for Education) and 35/92 (Welsh Office)*. London: CATE.

Creemers, Bert P. M. (1992) 'School Effectiveness, Effective Instruction and School Improvement in the Netherlands'. In Reynolds, David and Cuttance, Peter (eds.) *School Effectiveness*. London: Cassell.

Dearing, Ron (1993) *The National Curriculum and its Assessment, Final Report*. London: School Curriculum and Assessment Authority.

Department for Education (DfE) (1992) *Initial Teacher Training (Secondary Phase). Circular No 9/92*. London: DfE.

Department for Education (DfE) (1994) *Religious Education and Collective Worship. Circular No 1/94*. London: DfE.

Department of Education and Science (DES) (1989) *Discipline in Schools, (The Elton Report)*. London: HMSO.

Department of Education and Science (DES) (1990) *National Curriculum: English Key Stages Two To Four. Circular No. 2/94*. London: HMSO.

Education Reform Act (1988) London: HMSO.

Gillborn, David A., Nixon, Jon and Ruddock, Jean (1988) *Teachers'*

179

Experiences and Perceptions of Discipline in Ten Inner-City Comprehensive Schools. In *The Elton Report.*

Hagger, Hazel (1992) *The Role of the Training Institution in Mentor Development.* Paper presented at the UCET Annual Conference, November 1992, Oxford.

Kyriacou, Chris (2nd Edition 1997) *Essential Teaching Skills.* Stanley Thornes (Publishers) Ltd.

National Curriculum Council (1992) *Starting out with the National Curriculum. York*: NCC.

The Independent on Sunday (12 September 1993).
The Observer (1 May 1994).
The Times Educational Supplement (9 July 1992, 24 September 1993, 21 January 1994).
The Times Higher Education Supplement (18 February 1994).
Thio, Alex (1989) *Sociology: An Introduction* (Second Edition). New York: Harper & Row.
Thomas, Sally, Nuttall, Desmond L. and Goldstein, Harvey (1993) *AMA Project on Putting Examination Results in Context.* Institute of Education: University of London.
Trudgill, Peter (1975) *Accent, Dialect and the School.* London: Arnold.

Willis, Paul (1988) *Learning to Labour: How Working-Class Kids get Working-Class Jobs.* Aldershot: Gower.
Wragg, E.C. (1993) *Primary Teaching Skills.* London: Routledge.

Zehm, Stanley J. and Kottler, Jeffrey A. (1993) *On Being a Teacher: The Human Dimension.* Newbury Park, California: Corwin Press.

INDEX